KEEP
LEFT
REPAIRS · CARS FOR

# WILMSLOW & ALDERLEY EDGE

## A HISTORY & CELEBRATION

CLARE PYE

THE FRANCIS FRITH COLLECTION

www.francisfrith.co.uk

First published in the United Kingdom in 2005
by The Francis Frith Collection®

Hardback Edition 2005
ISBN 1-84589-222-4



British Library Cataloguing in Publication Data

Wilmslow & Alderley Edge - A History & Celebration
Clare Pye

The Francis Frith Collection
Frith's Barn, Teffont,
Salisbury, Wiltshire SP3 5QP
Tel: +44 (0) 1722 716 376
Email: info@francisfrith.co.uk
www.francisfrith.co.uk

Printed and bound in England

Front Cover: **ALDERLEY EDGE, VILLAGE SMITHY 1896** 37477t

Additional modern photographs by Clare Pye.

Domesday extract used in timeline by kind permission of
Alecto Historical Editions, www.domesdaybook.org
Aerial photographs reproduced under licence from
Simmons Aerofilms Limited.
Historical Ordnance Survey maps reproduced under licence from
Homecheck.co.uk

Every attempt has been made to contact copyright holders of illustrative material. We will be happy to give full acknowledgement in future editions for any items not credited. Any information should be directed to The Francis Frith Collection.

*The colour-tinting in this book is for illustrative purposes only, and is not intended to be historically accurate*

The map of lands belonging to John Trafford in 1771 (page 28) is used with the permission of Cheshire and Chester Archives and Local Studies Service. Records held by Cheshire and Chester Archives and Local Studies Service are reproduced with the permission of Cheshire County Council and Chester City Council and the owner/depositor to whom copyright is reserved.

AS WITH ANY HISTORICAL DATABASE, THE FRANCIS FRITH ARCHIVE IS CONSTANTLY BEING CORRECTED AND IMPROVED, AND THE PUBLISHERS WOULD WELCOME INFORMATION ON OMISSIONS OR INACCURACIES

# CONTENTS

**WILMSLOW FROM THE AIR 1955** AFR24909

**BC - Mesolithic Period**
Flint flakes show Alderley area was used for hunting

**1st Century**
Lindow Man (later nicknamed 'Pete Marsh') sacrificed in Lindow Moss

**2nd Century**
Romans mine lead on Alderley Edge

## Prehistory | Roman Britain | Dark Ages

**49BC**
Julius Caesar crosses the Rubicon

**AD79**
Eruption of Vesuvius destroying Pompeii

**AD122**
Emperor Hadrian orders Hadrian's Wall to be built

**AD455**
Vandals sack Rome

**AD520**
Possible period of King Arthur legend

**AD871**
King Alfred and Danelaw

**1598**
Perambulation of Alderley parish boundaries

**1642 - 49**
Civil War

**1660**
Thomas Stanley of Alderley awarded baronetcy

## Tudor Period | Stuart Britain

**1509**
Henry VIII becomes king

**1558**
Accession of Elizabeth 1

**1588**
Spanish Armada defeated

**1600**
Founding of East India Company

**1605**
Gunpowder Plot

**1649**
Charles I executed

**1666**
Great Fire of London

**1688-89**
Glorious Revolution

**1842**
Railway opens at Alderley 10 May 1842

**1857 - 78**
Alderley Edge Mining Company digs for copper and lead from the Edge

**1890s**
Sale of Trafford Park when the Manchester Ship Canal is built. The land becomes the world's first industrial estate

## Victorian Britain | Edwardian Era

**1837**
Victoria becomes queen

**1846**
Repeal of Corn Laws

**1851**
Great Exhibition at Crystal Palace

**1885**
Karl Benz designs first automobile

**1899-1902**
Boer War

**1901**
Queen Victoria dies

**1903**
Campaign for women's suffrage begins

**1910**
Edward VII dies

# HISTORICAL TIMELINE FOR WILMSLOW

## Middle Ages

**1066** Battle of Hastings. Norman rule begins

**1069-70** The harrying of the north; eastern Cheshire devastated

**1086** Two entries for Alderley in Domesday Book

**1086** Domesday Book

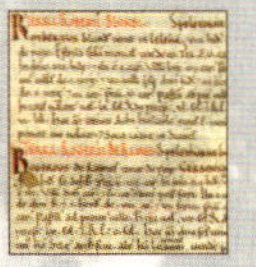

**1170** Murder of Thomas à Becket at Canterbury cathedral

**1215** Magna Carta

**1243** Arderne family granted charters for market at Alderley

**c1270** Roger Fitton is rector of Wilmslow

**1306** Robert the Bruce declares himself King of Scotland

## Late Medieval

**1328** Robert Byrom dies, first known incumbent of Alderley

**1348** Black Death kills 25 million in Europe

**Late 14th century** Chorley Old Hall probably built by William de Honford

**1415** Battle of Agincourt

**1485** Battle of Bosworth Field marks end of Plantaganet dynasty

## Georgian Era

**1739** John Wesley founds Methodist church

**1762** Mozart performs at the age of 6

**1784** Samuel Greg starts the Styal cotton-spinning mill

**1789** French Revolution

**1815** Battle of Waterloo

**1825** Stockton to Darlington Railway

**1830** The Liverpool to Manchester line opens, the first railway in the north west

## 20th Century Britain

**1914** First World War begins

**1925** Lyulph, 4th Lord Stanley, dies

**1926** John Logie Baird obtains first television picture

**1932** Alderley Park House burns down

**1939** Outbreak of Second World War

**c1950** Alderley Park bought by ICI, now Astra Zeneca.

**1956** Suez Crisis

**1966** England win World Cup

**1969** First man on the Moon

**1982** Falklands Conflict

**1995** Early 4th-century Roman coin hoard discovered in Engine Vein mineshaft

# PREFACE

STRUNG OUT ALONG the A34 are three distinct communities with their own unique characteristics; Wilmslow, Alderley Edge village and Nether Alderley. Wilmslow, built up round its old parish church, has all the trappings of a small town; Alderley Edge village is self-consciously a Victorian planned village, while Nether Alderley is the old village in Alderley parish. The latter place has a completely different history from the other two. They have been separate since Domesday: in different parishes, with different landowners and with a very different history.

Each community is proud of its own separate character, and it is impossible to treat them as one unit, at least until the Industrial Revolution, when they became linked not just by the main road, but the railway as well, which opened in 1842.

**ALDERLEY EDGE, THE VIEW FROM STORMY POINT c1955** A29023

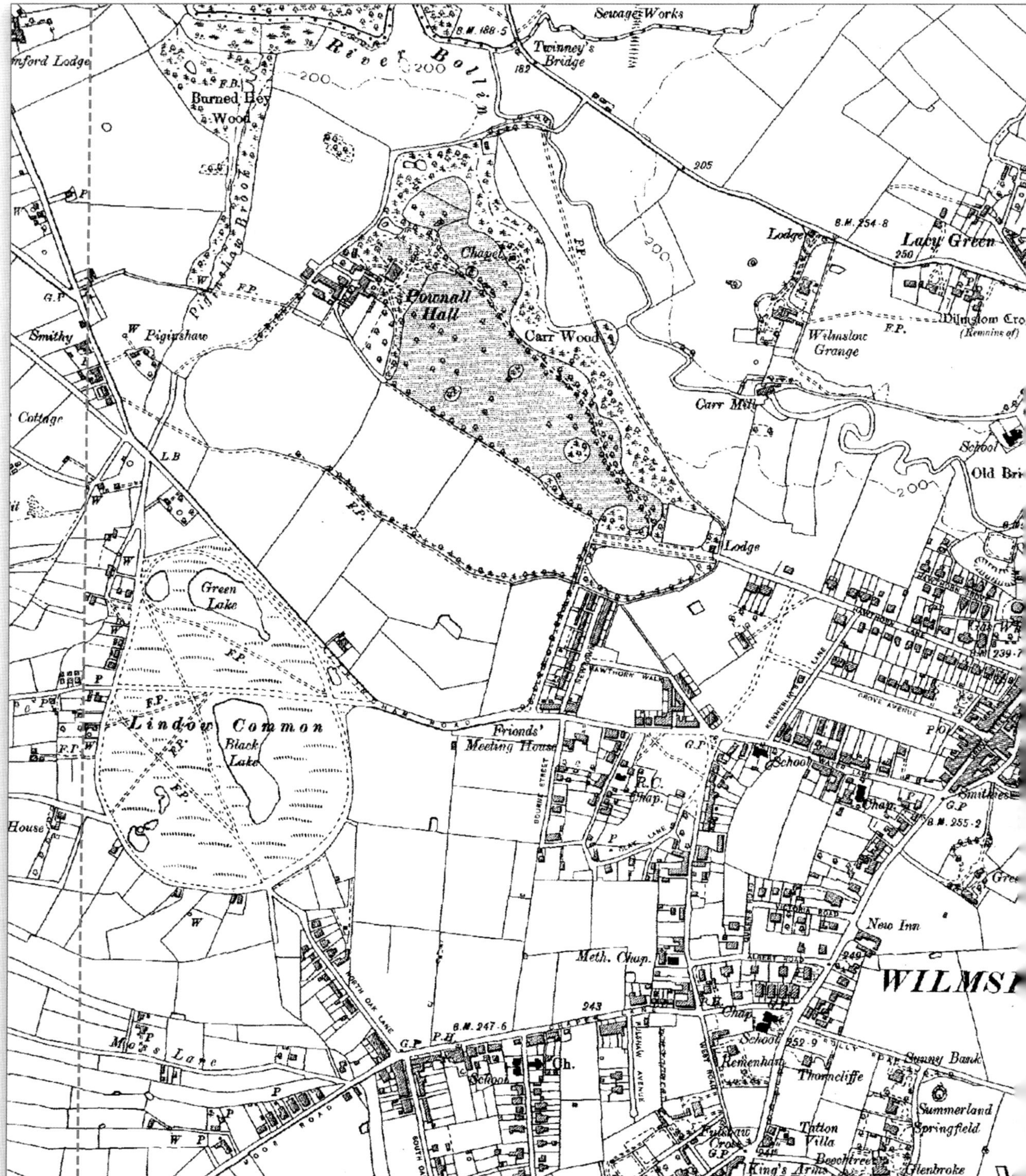
Sewage Works
River Bollin
Twinney's Bridge
Burned Hey Wood
Pigginshaw Brook
Lacy Green
Lodge
Chapel
Pownall Hall
Carr Wood
Wilmslow Grange
Wilmslow Cross (Remains of)
Carr Mill
School
Old Bri
Smithy
Pigginshaw
Cottage
Lodge
Green Lake
Lindow Common
Black Lake
Friends' Meeting House
R.C. Chap.
School
Smithies
New Inn
Meth. Chap.
WILMSL
Moss Lane
Ch.
School
Remenham
Thorncliffe
Sunny Bank
Summerland
Springfield
Tatton Villa
Beechtree
Glenbroke
King's Arms (P.H.)
Brookfield
Grove Avenue
Victoria Road
Albert Road
North Oak Lane
South Oak Lane
Bourne Street
Fulshaw Avenue
Hawthorn Lane
Hawthorn Walk
Kennerley's Lane

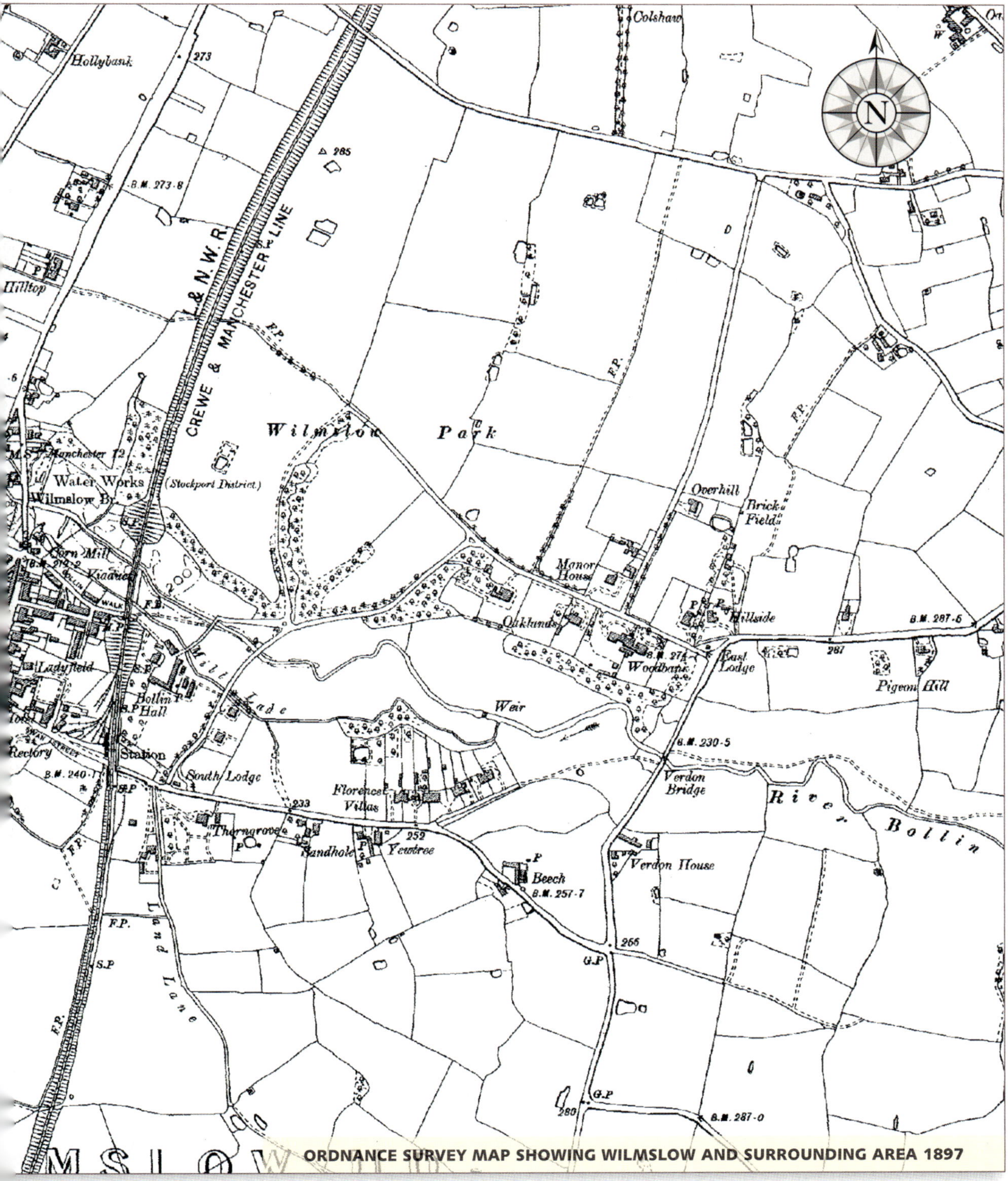

ORDNANCE SURVEY MAP SHOWING WILMSLOW AND SURROUNDING AREA 1897

CHAPTER ONE

# EARLY TIMES

TO GO BACK before the Norman Conquest, it is necessary to consider the area's early history as part of one inter-related landscape.

The earliest we can go back with any certainty is to Mesolithic times, and the people of that time who left traces of their hunting parties in the flint flakes that sometimes appear near Castle Rock on Alderley Edge. They must have used the rock as a viewpoint over the dense forest in the Bollin valley, looking for signs of game.

There is little of the Neolithic Age in the area. However, the Bronze Age is a different matter, for Alderley Edge is one of the most important sites in the country. People here had always believed that there had been ancient mining on the Edge. However, it was not until a wooden shovel, rescued by local author Alan Garner from the rubbish under the stage at Alderley Edge Primary School in the early 1950s, was dated in 1993 to the Early Bronze Age, 1850-1750 BC, that modern archaeology provided the scientific evidence. After this discovery the Manchester Museum and the National Trust conducted an excavation beside Engine Vein in 1997,

**Fact File**

*The oldest man-made artefacts on Alderley Edge are over 10,000 years old.*

ALDERLEY EDGE, THE VIEW FROM THE EDGE c1955 A29015

The view from Castle Rock, Alderley Edge, in about 1955.

The Engine Vein on Alderley Edge, the site of Early Bronze Age and Roman mining.

and carbon dating there fully confirmed what many people had long suspected. Alderley Edge is the site of the earliest known copper mine in England. The wooden shovel is now in Manchester Museum, though it is not yet on permanent display.

Bronze Age material has also been found in Wilmslow. When the railway was built in 1841-2, workmen found the remains of burial urns holding cremated bones when they dug the foundations for the viaduct over the Bollin. Unfortunately, these remains have disappeared. Modern engineering has also revealed evidence from this time. When the second runway was built at Manchester Airport, a Bronze Age settlement was revealed and excavated. All of these signs suggest a flourishing community in the area.

Moving on 1,800 years or so, and the Iron Age has left even grimmer reminders of itself in the remains of Lindow Man, who was sacrificed by the Celts in the 1st century AD. His body, offered to the gods, was left in the watery peat bog of Lindow Moss, a landscape on the borders of earth and water. He had been in the prime of life; the tribe had given of its best, perhaps to try and ward off the Romans who were invading Cheshire at this time. If that was so, then it was a futile and tragic effort to postpone the inevitable, as archaeological evidence nearby makes clear.

On Alderley Edge, the National Trust has an arrangement with the Derbyshire Caving Club to maintain the mines under the Edge. They are especially concerned with public safety. Consequently, in 1995, when a

## Fact File

*A bodiless head was found in the bog at Lindow. When it was discovered, the police first thought it was the head of a woman who had recently disappeared and got a confession to her murder out of her husband. The body was later found to date from the 1st century and had been preserved by the peat.*

suspicious saucer-shaped depression appeared beside Engine Vein, the DCC moved in to cap what everyone recognised was a collapsing mine shaft. Collapsing mine shafts become progressively more dangerous as the soil is removed, so they dug down very carefully. Four feet down the shaft they found a 4th-century Roman coin hoard, still in the broken pot in which it had been buried. It was not a high value hoard; analysis of the coins showed it probably represented a poor man's life savings, buried for safety at a time of political unrest, but never retrieved. One wonders what happened to the person who buried the pot but never came back to claim it.

The coins were early 4th-century AD, so anything below the coins should be older than that. Consequently, in 1997, at the same time as the Manchester Museum archaeologists were looking for the remains of Bronze Age mining at Engine Vein, they and the Caving Club excavated the shaft, now renamed Pot Shaft. A lot of lead mining spoil came out,

**ALDERLEY EDGE, STORMY POINT 2005** A29702k (Clare Pye)

Stormy Point, perhaps the most popular viewpoint on Alderley Edge.

## THE CAVING CLUB

The Derbyshire Caving Club have their own names for the shafts and tunnels in the mines under Alderley Edge. Balloon Shaft is so called because its depth was measured by floating a balloon up to the surface on a string.

with some Bronze Age hammer stones mixed up in it. 40 feet down they came to the bottom of the shaft and discovered that it linked with a short passage into Engine Vein itself. At the very bottom of Pot Shaft was a drainage sump, and in it, saturated with water, they found some oak planks. The wood was carbon dated, and it is clear that the planks date from the mid 1st century AD. Here was proof that as soon as the Romans conquered the Cheshire area, they were up on Alderley Edge mining the lead. Perhaps they hoped to find silver, as they had done in the Mendips, but even though there were no precious metals, the lead was extremely useful to the Romans, given their liking for good plumbing. More relevant locally, it probably provided the metal for the evaporating pans at the strategically important salt works a few miles away in Northwich and Middlewich.

After the Romans left Cheshire, the history of the area becomes rather murky. It is significant that almost all the place names in east Cheshire are Anglo-Saxon, which suggests the native British population, if it did not go away, was thoroughly absorbed into the dominant invader society and its language. Wilmslow means 'Wighelm's mound', while Alderley is 'Aldreth's clearing'. However Cheshire was border country; not for nothing does Mersey mean Border Water. Although officially in the Saxon kingdom of Mercia, Cheshire was distant from the power centre. To the north was the kingdom of Northumbria, while the Mersey estuary itself made the area vulnerable to Viking incursions. The odd clusters of Danish place names, for instance round Knutsford or in the Holmes Chapel area, suggests that the Northmen were trying to move in, particularly after they had been thrown out of Dublin by the Irish in the early 10th century.

### Fact File

*Alderley is named after a woman. Aldreth was a Saxon female name.*

It was at this time that Aethelflaed, the Lady of Mercia, reorganised the local government of Cheshire to defend the county against the invaders. This created the Hundred of Hamestan (later known as Macclesfield Hundred). Each hundred contained two parishes; Hamestan's were Prestbury and Cheadle. Both Wilmslow and Alderley were in Prestbury parish within the Hamestan hundred, although neither community appears to have been important either politically or economically. This humble situation was to become even worse in the years immediately after the Norman Conquest. In the winter of 1069-70, eastern Cheshire endured the devastation of the 'harrying of the north' - King William's revenge after a rebellion against his rule.

We are very lucky to have the Domesday Book, which was compiled by the Norman conquerors. It provides a remarkable snapshot into life in late 11th-century England. However, we have to remember why the survey was done: it was for taxation. William the Conqueror, now near the end of his reign, needed to know how much his vassals were worth, and how much he could get out of them. Consequently the organisation of the book is governed by the need to find out what the land and people were worth. Individual entries are not for communities, but rather individuals' holdings within each hundred. Places can appear twice. This applies to Alderley; one part, usually taken to be Nether Alderley, was held by Bigot of Loges, the other, probably Over Alderley, by William Fitz Nigel. The full entries are as follows:

## Fact File

*Aethelflaed was the daughter of King Alfred the Great. She married Aethelred, Earl of Mercia and ruled the earldom, which included Cheshire, after her husband died.*

***In Macclesfield Hundred***

*ALDERLEY. Bigot of Loges holds it.*
*Godwin held it as a free man. 1 hide paying tax.*
*Land for 4 ploughs. In lordship 1 (plough), with 2 ploughmen; 3 villagers and 1 rider with 1 plough.*
*Meadow, 1 acre; woodland 1 1/2 leagues long and 1 league wide; 2 enclosures.*
*Value before 1066, 20s; now 10s; found waste.*

***In Macclesfield Hundred***

*ALDERLEY William son of Nigel (William Fitzniel) holds it*
*William holds Alderley from the Earl. Brown held it; he was a free man. 1 hide paying tax. Land for 4 ploughs. It was and is waste.*
*Woodland 2 leagues long and 2 wide.*
*Value before 1066, 20s.*

The reference to 'waste', land that could be cultivated but was not under the plough in 1087, is a clue to the devastation of 20 years before. The area had still not recovered.

Wilmslow does not appear at all; the nearest places mentioned in Domesday, apart from Alderley, are Mottram and Mobberley. Neither place was worth very much, although Mottram was noted as having a hawk's eyrie, perhaps a sign that this was remote and unoccupied countryside. There are a number of reasons for this absence. Wilmslow may have been so unimportant that it was passed over, but it is more likely that, as with Cheadle, which was an important community, it was part of the Earl of Chester's holding of Macclesfield, and so included in that entry.

However, it is at this point that the fortunes of Alderley and Wilmslow start to divide, and it is necessary to explore their histories separately.

A SECTION OF A COUNTY MAP OF CHESHIRE SHOWING WILMSLOW AND SURROUNDING AREA c1850

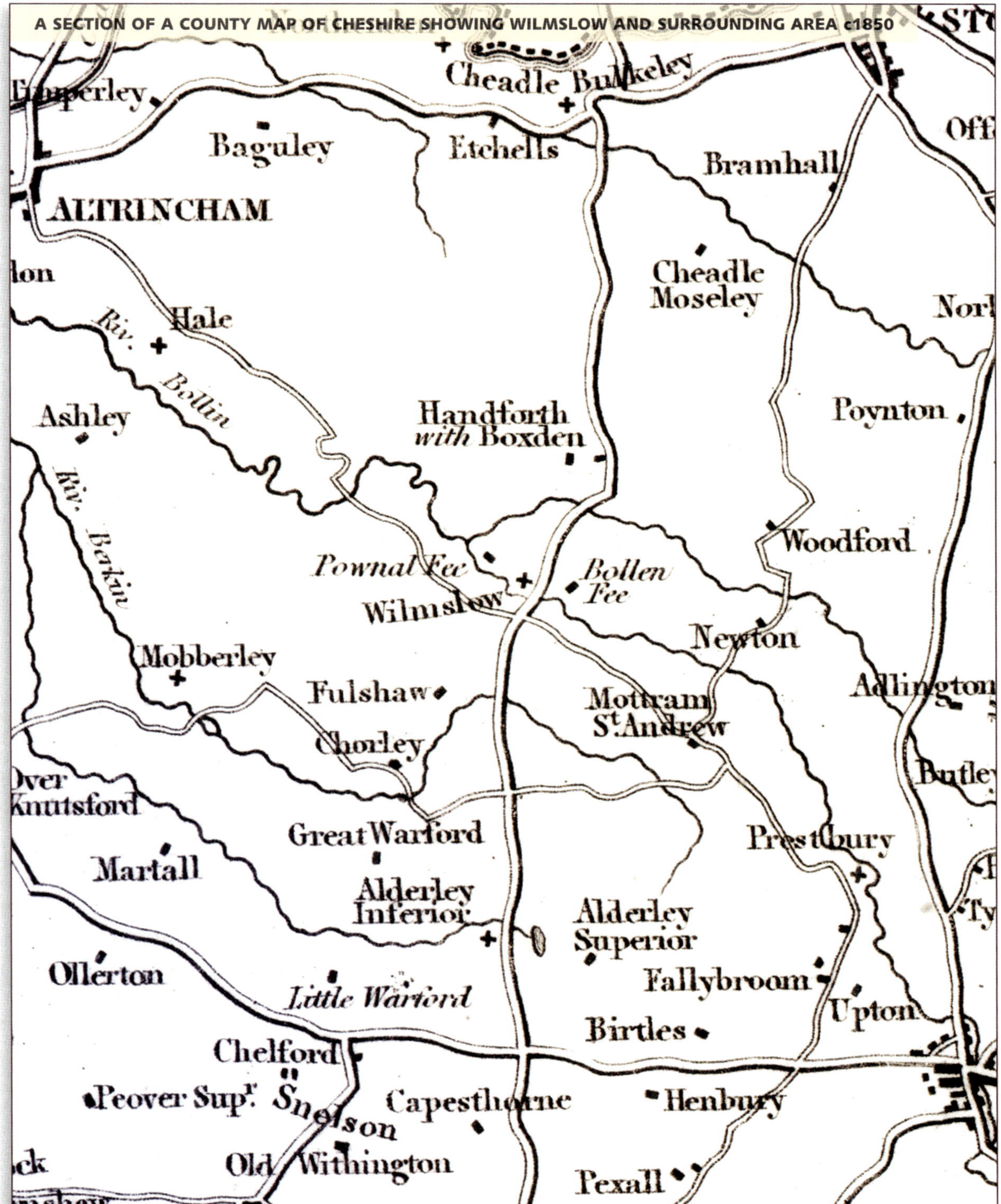

CHAPTER TWO

# WILMSLOW BEFORE THE INDUSTRIAL REVOLUTION

STRICTLY, WILMSLOW is just the name of the parish, and refers to the church and the immediate surroundings of the churchyard. The secular territorial areas, the townships and the medieval manors, were Fulshaw, Chorley, Bollin Fee and Pownall Fee, and these are the names that appear on the medieval charters.

The first mention we have from this area comes in a charter from the Earl of Chester to Richard de Fitton, some time in the late 12th century. This gave him the lordships of 'Fulschae, Chorleigh, Pounale, Morleigh, ... the wood of Ullersombe ... from the stream that comes from the Blake Lache of Shadow Moss and along the stream that runs into the Bollin, with the hamlets of Styhale, Curbichelegh and Northcliffe, Rylandis, Stanilondis, and Harethorne'. These names are recognisable today, even if the spelling

**Fact File**

*Prestbury means Priests' Town, a very suitable name for one of the country's largest parishes.*

**WILMSLOW, THE BOLLIN 2005** W103720k (Clare Pye)

Looking up the Bollin. The railway viaduct is in the background and the manorial mill used to be on the right bank of the river.

**WILMSLOW, THE BOLLIN FEE 2005** W103719k (Clare Pye)

This bar is one reminder of Wilmslow's original name, Bollin Fee.

is a bit different. The whole fief came to be known as Bollin, after the river that runs through it all. Now gone, swept away when the railway was built in the 19th century, there once was Bollin Hall, the home of the Fittons in the middle of their holding.

The Fittons were not content with possessing just the secular power in the area; they wanted to make sure they had power over all aspects of life. This meant they wanted to create their own parish. Then inside their own church they could have their own chapel, to house the dead members of the family and with a priest ready to say masses for their souls. They did not manage this until the late 13th century. However, by about 1270 Roger Fitton is recorded as being rector of Wilmslow, and in 1291 the tax assessment for all the parishes in England noted that Wilmslow was valued at £8, rather on the low side and only a third of the value of Prestbury.

One further ecclesiastical quirk happened in the early years of the Fittons. In the early 13th century, Richard de Fitton, the son of the first Lord of Bollin, gave Fulshaw to the Knights of St John of Jerusalem, one of the great fighting orders of monks that were so prominent in the history of the Crusades. Despite the loss of the Kingdom of Jerusalem in the late 12th century, crusading enthusiasm remained strong for the next 100 years or so. However a lawyer like Richard, aware of his responsibilities as Justiciar of Chester,

WILMSLOW, ST BARTHOLOMEW'S CHURCH 2005 W103721k (Clare Pye)

The chancel was rebuilt at the end of the 19th century, but original 16th-century windows can be seen nearer the tower.

probably thought a generous donation to Crusader funds was the best way for him to fulfil his religious and military obligations.

Wilmslow's parish church, dedicated to St Bartholomew, may have its origins in the 13th century, but the appearance of the main structure dates from the early 16th, just before the Reformation. The design is typical of East Cheshire churches built at this time; the style is Perpendicular, with a west tower to house the bells, a ring of six. The man responsible for this rebuilding was the rector of the day, Henry Trafford, who was the incumbent from 1516 to 1537, and is buried on the north side of the church near the altar. Many churches in north-east Cheshire underwent rebuilding

**Fact File**

*Cheshire churches typically have towers at the west end of the church rather than over the crossing.*

or had significant additions just before the Reformation, an indication that traditional religious life was still strong in this region.

However, St Bartholomew's was so thoroughly restored at various times in the second half of the 19th century that it takes an experienced architectural historian to untangle the evidence and say for sure what is medieval and what is Victorian. Nevertheless, like many churches, within its walls are clues to the history of past communities in the town. Among the features of medieval churches are the side chapels dedicated to the main landowners in the parish. In the north aisle is the Trafford chapel, and in the south aisle are the Booth and Hawthorne chapels. Throughout the church are memorials to prominent former inhabitants, including later ones to Samuel Greg, the builder of Styal Mill, and to John Prescott who was responsible for much of Wilmslow's development in the 19th century.

However, there is no Fitton chapel in Wilmslow church. If one wants to see Fitton memorials, then one has to go to Gawsworth, where a cadet branch of the family set itself up in the 14th century. This is because the main male line of the Fittons of Bollin died out around 1370, and Joanna Fitton, a great catch in her time, took Bollin with her as her dowry when she married Richard Venables, a younger son of the Kinderton Venables from

WILMSLOW, ST BARTHOLOMEW'S CHURCH FROM THE SOUTH 1896 37484

St Bartholomew's Church, Wilmslow, in 1896, before the chancel roof was heightened.

WILMSLOW, ST BARTHOLOMEW'S CHURCH, THE INTERIOR 1896 37485

Middlewich. Their son, William, inherited the Bollin estates and in turn had a son, Richard, and two daughters, Alice and Douce. When Richard died without any children to inherit, in about 1415, his sisters split the Bollin lands between them. Alice took most of Pownall Fee and parts of Chorley with her when she married Sir Edmund Trafford of Trafford. Douce took Bollin Fee, Styal and the mill in Pownall as her dowry when she married Sir William Booth, the head of the family that later came to own Dunham Massey. This last couple are both buried under a superb brass before the altar rails in Wilmslow church. Holding hands, Sir William is in plate armour with a greyhound at his feet, and Douce has a smaller dog at hers. Dogs are symbols of fidelity in heraldry, so perhaps it is not fanciful to suppose Douce and William were happily married.

St Bartholomew's Church is all that can easily be identified as part of the old manorial centre of Bollin Fee. Bollin Hall itself went when the railway came through in the 1840s, but it had long been a working farmhouse rather than a gentleman's residence. The site of the mill by the Bollin can be identified by modern place names, but United Utilities' water treatment works on the opposite side of the river is a poor substitute for what had

WILMSLOW, FROM THE RAILWAY VIADUCT 1897 39601

A view of Wilmslow from the railway viaduct, taken in 1897. The three-storey building in the foreground is Wilmslow's old corn mill, and the mill leat from the Bollin can still be seen.

WILMSLOW, MILLBANK HOUSE 2005
W103702k (Clare Pye)

Only place names survive as a reminder of the site of Wilmslow's corn mill.

been there before, essential though it is to Wilmslow's public health.

The two families, the Traffords and the Booths, held the manors and most of the lands in Wilmslow until the 19th century. However, they were both absentee landlords, and as the years went on, they tended to look on their lands here, not so much as their homes, but as sources of their income. Their absence also meant that other families emerged from under their shadow, and it is these families

**Fact File**

*Trafford Park, the home of the Trafford family, was sold in the 1890s when the Manchester Ship Canal was built. The area became the first industrial estate in the world.*

**ALDBOROUGH, A MAP OF LANDS IN THE TOWNSHIPS OF HOUGH AND CHORLEY BELONGING TO JOHN TRAFFORD ESQR 1771** ZZZ05393 (Reproduced by kind permission of Cheshire and Chester Archives and Local Studies Service)

The de Trafford estate map of Chorley (modern Alderley Edge village) in the early 1770s.

who are responsible for building the old halls that are still embedded in the modern suburban landscape, in particular, Chorley Hall, Hawthorn Hall and Pownall Hall. Bollin Hall and old Fulshaw Hall have gone but the others are still with us

Chorley Old Hall is the oldest secular building in Wilmslow. The stone hall, which has still got its cross passage, was probably built by William de Honford, a member of the Handforth family of Handforth Hall, in the late 14th century, on a fashionable moated site. Moats were symbols, if not of actual gentility, then certainly of aspirations to gentry status. They reached the height of popularity in the 14th century and are very common in Cheshire, as they are easy to make on the flat clay lands of the Cheshire Plain. They are the medieval equivalent of remote controlled gates. Access to the house was limited to one entrance over the bridge, and this was enough to keep out undesirable chancers, but in all honesty, they were not formidable defensive structures capable of repelling a determined enemy, and there are few records of these moated houses being involved in serious fighting for very long.

The half-timbered wing at Chorley was built in the 16th century by later owners, the Davenports, a branch of the Bramhall family. In the early 17th century William Davenport sold the hall and its lands, and in 1640 they were purchased by Thomas Stanley of Alderley. The Stanleys let the hall and adjacent lands to farmers, and it remained a working farm until after the Second World War.

**ALDERLEY EDGE, CHORLEY HALL c1955** A29010

Chorley Old Hall, Alderley Edge village, when it was still a farmhouse.

Hawthorne Hall, Wilmslow, in 1897. The hall was originally in the hamlet of Morley.

While Chorley Old Hall is still recognisable for what it was, and lies, still with its moat, on the outskirts of Alderley Edge village, Hawthorn Hall, originally part of the hamlet of Morley, is embedded in Wilmslow's residential development. The extent of the house's influence can be read in all the Hawthorn place names in the immediate area: Hawthorn Lane, Street, Walk, and Grove, Hall Road, and the Park Road that used to lead down to the original park round the hall. Peering through the now ferocious security gates, it is possible to see that the hall, with its multiple gables, is similar to Saltersford Hall out by Lindow Moss; they were probably built about the same time in the 17th century. Walking round the area, one can track the gradual encroachment of suburbia on the hall and its park, from the 19th century three-storey semis and 1930s detached villas to the post-war semi-detached houses in Hawthorn Lane and the eventual development of the hall itself. The property passed through a number of hands and never seems to have been in one family for very long. In the 19th century, the hall itself was used as a school.

Pownall Hall was also in Morley hamlet, but, thanks to the present school's sports field, it still has its immediate park, although, like Hawthorn Hall, its fields have almost all been built on. Most of this development dates from between the wars, and amidst the obvious developers' standard designs are some striking Art Deco houses, very modern for their times.

In the early Middle Ages the de Pownall family took their name from the hall, but they seem to have been farmers rather than

**WILMSLOW, POWNALL HALL 2005** W103703k (Clare Pye)

Pownall Hall, once one of Wilmslow's halls, is now a flourishing preparatory school.

landowners. A cadet branch of the Fittons lived here until the late 15th century, when Ellen Fitton married Humphrey Newton. However, in the late 1820s the estate was purchased by a Liverpool merchant, a James Pownall, who claimed descent from the original de Pownalls. He proceeded to knock down the old hall and build himself a modern house on the site. It is this house that forms the core of the present edifice, though it is heavily disguised under the transformation achieved by Henry Boddington. He bought Pownall in 1883, commissioning Henry Ball to extend the house and the Century Guild to design the interior as a superb example of the Arts and Crafts style, with de Morgan tiles and Shrigley and Hunt windows.

Old Fulshaw Hall has gone: the house in the middle of the new office development is

**WILMSLOW, AN ART DECO HOUSE 2005**
W103704k (Clare Pye)

An Art Deco house near Pownall Hall, part of Wilmslow's residential expansion between the wars.

Pownall Hall, Wilmslow, when it was still a private house.

Victorian and the park on the other side of the main road was developed for villas in the 19th century. The Finneys were the last family to live in the original hall, originally a merchant family, who settled in the area in the early 17th century and bought the hall in 1682. One of them, Samuel Finney, was enamel painter to Queen Charlotte, George III's wife, and wrote a history of the Wilmslow area. His descendant, Peter Davenport Finney, a young don in Oxford, is buried in Wilmslow Church, having died suddenly in 1824 on his way home from Sidmouth. After this, the estate passed through a number of hands and the land was eventually sold for housing after the railway arrived. The park was set out for substantial villas, rather on the lines of the development that had just taken place in Alderley Edge village. The last phase of development in this area was the building of the Refuge Insurance offices when they moved out of Manchester. Since then the series of takeovers and amalgamations in the insurance world has meant that the site is looking for new occupiers at the moment.

By the end of the Middle Ages the Wilmslow area was a solidly prosperous farming community, but with no great family acting as a focus for the inhabitants. The Reformation brought some changes; the manor of Fulshaw no longer belonged to the Knights of St John, and the Traffords' decision in the 1630s to return to the old Catholic faith meant they lost the right to present rectors to St Bartholomew's Church. Being Catholic, they were naturally on the Royalist side in the Civil War, but Wilmslow itself fell very largely under Parliamentary control during the conflict. The Booths, who fought for Parliament, owned much of the land, and the Parliamentary commander Sir Henry Brereton lived just up the road in Handforth. There was a skirmish at Finneys Bridge in 1643 and the Parliamentary leader, Colonel Dukinfield, paid a most unwelcome visit to the rector, Thomas Wright, during which some of the rector's servants were killed and valuables were stolen.

## NONCONFORMISM

Between 1665 and 1689, both Catholicism and Protestant nonconformism were penalised by the government. Everyone was supposed to go to Anglican services in the parish church, or else they lost many political rights.

WILMSLOW, THE RECTORY 1897 39612

Wilmslow rectory was built in the late 18th century, after all the disturbances of the Civil War had been settled. No longer a rectory, it is now a restaurant.

In 1645 old Thomas Wright was ejected from the living, presumably because of his known Royalist sympathies and his refusal to give up using the Anglican Book of Common Prayer. A Puritan preacher, John Brereton, probably a relation of the Parliamentary commander, was put in his place. Apparently the Puritans demolished the organ, sold the silver and presented Mr Brereton with a pewter basin to baptise the congregation. He in his turn was expelled in 1660, and Thomas Wright came back, just for one year, as he died in 1661.

**WILMSLOW, DEAN ROW CHAPEL 1897** 39619

However in the late 17th century this part of Cheshire tended to be very radical in its religious views. The congregation at Ringway chapel, not far away from Wilmslow, persisted in holding illegal meetings after the Restoration, and some of them even became Quakers. The Independent chapel at Dean Row is one of a number of similarly designed chapels in the area. They were all built in the early 1690s, as soon as the Act of Toleration of 1689 allowed Dissenters to build chapels, and reveals how strong the nonconformist tradition was in this part of the world.

The design of these chapels, with their plain and simple pews in full view of the pulpit, show they were intended for the congregation to hear the word of the Lord without any distractions. The gallery is reached from an outside stair. There is a tradition that a lookout always stood at the top of these stairs in case the authorities wanted to stop the services. This may have applied to the original Ringway chapel in the 1660s, when the Anglican Sir Peter Leicester of Tabley was vigorously pursuing the Puritans. However, in the 1690s, when the Dissenters' worship was quite legal, the outside stair was probably to make it easier for the congregation to get to and from their seats without taking up valuable space downstairs.

Until the Industrial Revolution, Wilmslow was largely a collection of farming hamlets round the old parish church. The absence of any great landowning family living in the parish after the departure of the Fittons, meant that the area lacked a headquarters to provide a focus for development. However, this very lack of a dominant landowner meant that it was relatively easy for changes to be made.

CHAPTER THREE

# NETHER ALDERLEY BEFORE THE INDUSTRIAL REVOLUTION

NETHER ALDERLEY, or just Alderley, as it was known until the mid 19th century, has a separate history from Wilmslow. Different parishes and different landowners both mean a different story.

By the 13th century Alderley was owned by the Arderne family. Although the family headquarters were on the other side of the county at Aldford, like many landowners of the time the Ardernes were intent on exploiting the commercial potential of their estates. In 1243, the Ardernes were granted charters to establish markets at both Alderley and Aldford. In Alderley they had the right to hold a weekly market on Saturdays and an annual fair in August at the time of the feast of St Lawrence. The plans for a market did not succeed, as both Knutsford and Congleton already had established markets on a Saturday, and Macclesfield had a Monday market. The Cross, beside the junction of Congleton Road and Welsh Row, is perhaps the only reminder of this failed speculation. However the community of Alderley parish continued to hold their Wakes in the second or third week of August. Until the mid 19th century the celebrations were centred on St Mary's Church, Nether Alderley, after which they moved up the Edge to the Wizard Inn. After the move, the date of the Wakes changed to Easter but they continued to be held until the outbreak of war in 1939.

**NETHER ALDERLEY, ST MARY'S CHURCH 2005**

N148701k (Clare Pye)

## Fact File

*Small oval churchyards, such as the one at Nether Alderley, are thought to be a sign of an early Christian community.*

The timing of the fair to St Lawrence-tide reflects the original dedication of St Mary's Church, Nether Alderley; the date of the market charter, 1243, suggests strongly that a chapel of ease had already been built in the village before the independent parish of Alderley was created. In an age of bad winter roads, the dead weight of a coffin could not be easily taken over the Edge to the mother church at Prestbury. There may have been a very early place of worship at Alderley, where there is an oval churchyard and the remains of an old preaching cross. The great yew tree there has been dated as over 1,200 years old. However, the first record of an incumbent priest in Alderley is the record of the death of Robert Byrom in 1328, and it is now generally accepted that the parish itself dates from 1300.

St Mary's Church is an interesting mixture. The oldest existing part is the 14th century nave. However, this shows signs of expansion later, in alterations in the windows in the clerestory. The south porch is 15th-century, but there is evidence of it being moved to its present position when the tower was built in the early 16th century. This was almost certainly built by Richard Plat, the mason who was responsible for Mobberley church tower, erected at the same time. The chancel was rebuilt by the Stanleys in the 1850s to house the tomb of the 1st Lord Stanley, but it may have replaced an even older 13th-century structure.

## Fact File

*Recently, the parish of Over Alderley and Birtles has been reunited with Nether Alderley and Great Warford to recreate the original parish of Alderley. This explains why Alderley parish has three churchwardens, one for each township.*

Nut Tree Farm in Welsh Row in 1896.

The new parish of Alderley comprised three townships, Nether and Over Alderley and Great Warford. Parish boundaries usually follow obvious physical features, such as the Pott Brook boundary on the north side of Over Alderley, but where there are no such obvious demarcations, any deviation can provide an insight into the area at this time. In particular there is an anomaly in the boundary between Nether Alderley and Chorley in Alderley Edge village where a tongue of Alderley land comes down off the Edge to the A34. The large bank of this boundary can still be seen by the Congleton Road in St Hilary's Park; indeed, when the planning permission for the housing development was given in 1999 it was conditional on preserving the remains of this bank. Where one finds boundary anomalies like this, the usual reason is that they are respecting a pre-existing developed feature. The archaeological survey at the time of the St Hilary's development was unable to date the bank but did reveal evidence of medieval iron working, so perhaps this is what was at issue.

Although the classic three-field system of agriculture was rare in Cheshire, it was not uncommon for townships to share a common field, at least in the early Middle Ages. Field name evidence in the Alderley area, from the 1841 tithe map, such as 'Town Field Gate' and 'Church Field', suggests common fields around the centre of the township, although by the end of the Middle Ages, these had disappeared. Like Wilmslow, Nether Alderley showed a typical field pattern of enclosed fields round farmsteads, and the houses grouped in small hamlets. As in Wilmslow there were a number of subsidiary halls, notably Heawoods and Soss Moss Halls. However, unlike Wilmslow, we can still see evidence of the manorial centre to the community in the village of Nether Alderley, with its church, mill, manor house and one-time inn.

## ST HILARY S PARK

The preserved bank on the south side of the drive into St Hilary's Park may be the oldest man-made feature in Alderley Edge village, as it could date back to Saxon times.

### Fact File

*Common names for fields taken in from common land are 'Common Piece' and 'Intake' or 'Intack'.*

Up on the Edge itself, there is another anomaly in the township boundary between Nether and Over Alderley. Coming south from Saddlebole, the boundary follows the Edge until the Golden Stone, strikes straight across the shared common land, then curves round to Finlow Hill Lane. It then deviates, following the field boundaries south of Mottram House, where it makes a series of sharp turns until it runs south east, past

Hayman's Farm to Alderley Park, where it again deviates round the park boundary until it reaches and follows the stream. The last deviation implies a park had already been created before 1300 and the sharp changes of direction on the top of Finlow Hill suggest enclosures already existed before 1300.

Certainly, by the time we can investigate manor and parish records in the 16th century, we see a typical Cheshire landscape of separate holdings and enclosed fields with areas of common heath and moss land. Soss Moss, Sandle Heath, Monks Heath, Broadheath and, in particular, Alderley Edge are all important areas of common land within Alderley parish. The common on the Edge had a typical concave outline with tracks and paths creating funnel shapes as they come on to the heath. There were probably no defined tracks at this time across the common land; people would come up on to the Edge and then strike out across it to their destination. In the 16th century, the common land of Over Alderley extended eastwards into Broadheath. The Stanleys and the Leycesters of Tabley were the two main landowners in Over Alderley by this time, and they had an acrimonious legal wrangle from 1598 to 1661 over common rights in the parish. The smallholdings and enclosures in Slade Lane and School Lane along the boundary between the two estates are probably encroachments on the common land allowed by the landowners as they helped to define their respective territories.

The Stanley involvement with Alderley goes back to the early 15th century, but

NETHER ALDERLEY, ARTISTS LANE 1896 37460

This is one of the old roads from the fields of the Cheshire Plain up on to the Edge.

## MOTTRAM HOUSE

Mottram House used to be known as Cuckoo's Nest in the early 20th century, when three of the Barber family of Brynlow Hill lived there.

has a complicated history as the family has a number of branches. In the mid 14th century, the Arderne family split the land in Alderley between two brothers; the elder, John, inherited most of Nether Alderley together with the rest of the Arderne lands in Cheshire; the younger son, Peter, got Fernhill in Nether Alderley and land in Over Alderley. Peter's great-grand-daughter and heiress, Margaret, married Richard Weever, and their descendant, Elizabeth Weever, married John Stanley, the elder brother of the 1st Earl of Derby, in the mid 15th century, bringing the Over Alderley and Weever lands with her as her dowry. This branch of the Stanleys managed their lands in Over and Nether Alderley from their main house at Weever during most of the 16th century. They married respectably endowed women from the local gentry, and generally established themselves in the area. In the late 16th century, Thomas Stanley, who died in 1591, decided to transfer the headquarters of his estates from Weever to Alderley and built the Elizabethan part of Alderley Old Hall, including the service block, which was saved from the 1779 fire and is still standing. He was the first of his family to describe himself 'of Alderley and Weever', rather than the other way round and he is buried in St Mary's in the south aisle. His grandson, another Thomas, inherited the estate in 1595.

**NETHER ALDERLEY 2005** N148702k (Clare Pye)

The schoolroom, church and rectory in Nether Alderley are still very much as the Stanleys would have known it.

## Fact File

*John Stanley's only son was killed in an accident before 1500 when a tennis ball hit him in the eye.*

Meanwhile, the elder branch of the Arderne family also ended with a female heiress. John of Arderne's daughter, Matilda, had married a Sir Thomas Stanley in the early 15th century, and this branch of the Stanleys held Nether Alderley with the rest of the Arderne inheritance for the next 100 years. However, the John Stanley who held the land in the late 15th century, faced with the problem of splitting the estate between

NETHER ALDERLEY, THE MILL DAM 2005 N148703k (Clare Pye)

The mill dam behind Nether Alderley Mill also created the moat for the Old Hall, which was on an island on the right.

three daughters, sold the reversion of his lands to his cousin, Sir William Stanley of Holt. Unfortunately Sir William, backing the wrong side during Perkin Warbeck's rebellion in 1495, was attainted on his execution two years later, and his estates were confiscated by the Tudors. Consequently, when John Stanley died in 1508 his lands escheated to the Crown. Alderley was granted to Sir William Brereton in the early 1530s, but reverted back to the Crown when he too fell foul of Tudor politics in 1536. 20 years later, the Crown sold the lordship of the manor of Nether Alderley to Sir Edward Fitton of Gawsworth, and it was the Fittons who in 1602 sold the lands and lordship of Nether Alderley to Thomas Stanley of Over Alderley for £2,000.

This sale by the Fittons ended another quarrel amongst the local gentry. Although he did not own the lordship of the manor, when old Thomas Stanley had moved his family to Nether Alderley he was Nether Alderley's greatest landowner. He wanted to demonstrate his position in the parish, so he built a private pew for himself in the church. This was resented by the Fittons. Although they never attended St Mary's on Sunday, having a perfectly good church of their own

## STANLEY PALACE

Sir Peter Warburton, Chief Justice of Chester, built a town house in Chester which came to the Stanleys when his daughter Elizabeth married Thomas Stanley. It was renamed Stanley Palace, and is now the offices of the English Speaking Union in Watergate in Chester.

in Gawsworth, they thought Thomas Stanley was getting above himself. The Fittons had the pew destroyed, and the case landed in the church courts at Chester. Young Thomas Stanley, the grandson, was able to settle the quarrel when he bought out the Fitton interest in Alderley; he used some of his wife's assets to pay for this (Elizabeth Stanley's father, Peter Warburton, had amassed a legal fortune as Chief Justice of Chester). Stanley's position was consolidated when he was knighted in 1603 by James I.

**NETHER ALDERLEY, THE STAIRS TO THE STANLEY PEW, ST MARY'S CHURCH 2005** N148705k (Clare Pye)

The stairs to the first-floor Stanley pew in St Mary's Church were outside the church.

**NETHER ALDERLEY, THE STANLEY COAT OF ARMS 2005** N148704k (Clare Pye)

The Stanley coat of arms with its eagle and child crest. The 4th Lord Stanley's coat of arms appears on his mausoleum in St Mary's churchyard.

However, the quarrel may help to explain the peculiar design of the Stanley pew. Elevated above the nave like a Jacobean opera box, it has to be reached by an outside stair. Once it would have had a direct view of the pulpit, which used to be further west than it is now. The design also reflects the religious changes of the Reformation. Families of the gentry no longer needed separate aisles to house their private chapels with a priest to say masses for their souls. They needed comfortable seating to listen to the long sermons that were such a feature of 17th-century religious life.

Unfortunately, Sir Thomas Stanley died at the age of 29 in 1606, only three years after he was knighted. His widow remarried and she kept the Alderley lands as her dower until her death in 1631, so it was not until then that her son, also a Thomas Stanley, came to live in Alderley with his young wife, Elizabeth Pyte, who came from Worcestershire. It was from his father-in-law's park that Thomas took beech mast for his park in Alderley, the ancestors of all the beech trees in the Alderley area.

## BEECH TREES

Alderley's great beech trees, with their smooth grey bark, were favourite places for the Stanleys to carve their names and their future spouses' names when they got engaged to be married. The trees, descendants of those planted so long ago by Sir Thomas Stanley, were nearly all cut down for timber during the Second World War.

This Thomas pursued a prudent course through the troubled years of the mid 17th century. Appointed to the bench when he was quite young, he was made sheriff of the county in 1631, and would have been responsible for collecting taxes for the Crown and organising Parliamentary elections. However, by 1640, he had become vociferous in his opposition to Charles I's Ship Money tax, and in the Civil Wars that broke out two years later, he was part of the Parliamentary leadership in Cheshire, serving especially on the Monthly Assessment Committee which raised taxes for the Parliamentary side. The royalist historian, Clarendon, had to admit that the Cheshire parliamentary leaders executed their responsibilities 'with notable sobriety and indefatigable industry'. As part of the original moderate leadership of the county, siding with old George Booth of Dunham Massey against the more hard line local army leader, William Brereton of Handforth, Stanley disliked the military radicals who emerged towards the end of the first Civil War. The correspondence between Stanley and Brereton shows the latter desperate for money to pay the troops, while Stanley argued he could not tax the county any harder; the people 'are so far exhausted betwixt free quartering of our own and plundering by the enemy'.

Although the war officially ended in 1646, the Parliamentary army was kept in force pending a constitutional settlement. The soldiers did not receive their arrears of pay, and in May 1647 an army detachment occupied Alderley Hall until they were paid off with £50. In July the moderate gentry, including Stanley, were rounded up by the soldiers and imprisoned in Chester until money was found to pay them. Chester was just emerging from an appalling siege and an outbreak of plague the year before, and the room where the magistrates were imprisoned lacked even the basic amenities of sanitation, so with much protest they quickly gave in to the soldiers' demands, issuing promissory notes on their own recognisances.

During the crisis of the second Civil War and the king's trial and execution Stanley kept a low profile, but was sufficiently in favour with the new regime to be a magistrate by March 1649, again involved in running the county, especially on the financial side. He was a diligent local magistrate, prominent in organising the new civil marriages that were introduced in 1653. The parish records for St Mary's Church include several of these; apparently notice was given either by posting banns in the church porch or by announcing them at market day in Macclesfield. During Booth's Rising in 1659, Stanley went into hiding. Whether this was to avoid arrest by the insurgents or merely to see what the outcome would be before committing himself we do not know, but he was sufficiently under suspicion to be called to London for questioning in 1660, after the Restoration. Still, Thomas Stanley kept his seat on the bench and even emerged with a baronetcy from Charles II, the first Cheshire man to be so honoured in 1660, probably because the king recognised his long administrative experience in the county and fundamental acceptance of the realities of power. Royalists, such as Peter Leycester, who also became a baronet at this time, were quite disgusted at the honour done to their old enemy. Leycester, though, got some satisfaction in having his family's long-running dispute with the Stanleys concerning manorial rights in Over Alderley decided in his favour, mostly, as he admitted, because the judge was also a Royalist!

Looking at the situation at St Mary's Church at this time, Sir Thomas's Puritan sympathies are evident. In 1630 Samuel Shipton, the son of the previous rector, was presented to the living. He was an Oxford don at Brasenose, where he had tutored Peter Leycester. In 1643 he was ejected from the living as a supporter of the king and Nicholas Steventon became rector. Steventon's religious affiliations are clear to see as he signed the Presbyterian Attestation of Cheshire Ministers in 1648, and he was himself thrown out of the living in 1660 when Shipton returned. However, Steventon must have been canonically ordained as he was compensated with the living of St Mary on the Hill near Chester. After Shipton died in 1670, James, Sir Thomas's fourth son, already rector of Mobberley, became rector. However, he survived only another four years and is buried in his old parish. His widow, Elizabeth Byron of Macclesfield, left money on her death in 1703 to the minister of the nonconformist chapel in King Edward Street, which had been her customary place of worship for many years.

During all these vicissitudes, the community of Alderley continued its traditional way of life. The Court leet records from the late 16th to the early 18th century reveal an active, self-regulating community, well aware of the individual's rights and responsibilities within it and pursuing the parish's customary rights and obligations. One of the fullest early records comes from 1598, when the Fittons still held the manor. The court was concerned that everyone contributed to the upkeep of the parish pinfold (animal pound) up at the

Butts near the boundary of the common on the Edge. It also worried about sheep worrying, dogs out of control, affrays between villagers, the rights of turbary (digging turf) on Soss Moss, the repair of highways and the licensing of marl-pits. These are typical concerns of any Court leet, but in 1598, the jurors were especially concerned with defining the parish boundaries up on the Edge and with inspecting the 'new-builded' mill. Nether Alderley mill is an Elizabethan building, but it is a rebuild of a 14th-century structure. They appointed a time in Whitsun week to deal with both matters.

**NETHER ALDERLEY, THE MILL 2005** N148706k (Clare Pye)

Nether Alderley mill dates from the Middle Ages. It is now owned by the National Trust.

**NETHER ALDERLEY, INSIDE THE MILL 2005**

ZZZ05394 (Clare Pye)

Machinery inside Nether Alderley mill.

**NETHER ALDERLEY, THE GOLDENSTONE 2005**

N148707k (Clare Pye)

The Goldenstone is the boundary or mere stone dividing Over and Nether Alderley's parts of the Edge.

**ALDERLEY EDGE, THE MERE STONE, SADDLEBOLE 2005** A29704k

The parish boundary or mere stone at the top of Saddlebole bank is marked with a cross.

**ALDERLEY EDGE, SADDLEBOLE 2005**

A29703k (Clare Pye)

The estate boundary on Saddlebole on Alderley Edge may date back to Saxon times.

When the parish came to inspect the parish boundaries, they followed a route that can still be traced today. It is worth reproducing this in full as it provides the first written record of many of the landscape features on the Edge:

'On Thursday Whitsun week, as before rehearsed, the jury did walk the meres on Alderley Edge and did begin at Findlow Hill, the mere there and so to the great stone and so to the mere-stone at the bottom of the sides of the old ditch and so up the old ditch to another mere-stone which many of the jury do remember stood on the end and is now fallen down. From thence to the great mere-stone in the intake and so from that stone straight through to another stone in the bottom near the pit on the commons that Lingard had marl out of. And so lineally by the mere-stone to the top of the bank near Lingard's house and so to a great stone called the Golden Stone on the north side of the wain way that cometh from Lingards to the Beacon. And so lineally to a little mere-stone in the track way towards the mineholes and so to the mere-stone at the top of the hill and from thence on the north side the minehole directly to the Saddlebole and so from the Saddlebole along under the great stones after the crest. And so back after the crest by the great stones to the two stones lying together over against the irongates hanging stone on the slack and from the hanging stone after the crest up the [ ] towards the Beacon to a stone lying in the same siche. And so following the hill side from crest to crest as they show themselves to the Castle Stone and so along after the crest of the Castle Stone and from thence after the crest all along the hill to a stone that lyeth in the slack which is reputed the merestone towards Chorley beneath the great quarry. And so from that stone turning south westward to the hedge between the lane and the inheritance of Sir Edward Fitton in the holding of Reginald Finlow and the lands of Edward Trafford Esq in the holding of [ ]. All of which several meres and mere-stones the jury do find and agree by relation of witnesses and the ancient knoledge and reports of those amongst them to be the

**ALDERLEY EDGE, IRONGATES 2005**

A29713k (Clare Pye)

These are the two great stones which are mentioned in the 1598 perambulation. Some people think these are the Iron Gates of the Alderley legend (discussed on page 67).

ALDERLEY EDGE, THE BEACON 1896 37465

The beacon's bricks and the conical top date from the late 18th century.

true meres of Nether Alderley on Alderley edge and no other between Nether Alderley and Over Alderley, Nether Alderley and the Hough and Chorley.'

The mineholes referred to were probably Pillar Mine and the Devil's Grave on Stormy Point.

A siche is a ditch, a wain way is a wagon way and a merestone is a boundary stone; the reference to 'mineholes' is the earliest written evidence of mining on the Edge. They were clearly recognised and long-standing landmarks, but there is no reference in the Court leets at this time to mining actively happening. Some of the existing mineholes on the Edge are thought to be medieval. The hanging stone was above Holy Well; according to old men interviewed by John Stanley about 1800, it fell down in 1740, making the houses nearby shake with the impact. There is a legend that an old woman and her cow are buried beneath it.

It is also possible, by reading the Court leet records, to follow families though the generations. The Mottersheads were long-time tenants on Brynlow, at what is now known as White Barn Farm. Reynold Mottershead was paid 6 shillings in 1534 for looking after a couple of stray horses found on the Edge. Reginald or Randle Mottershead appears in the Court leets frequently about 1600; he appears to have followed his own

ALDERLEY EDGE, THE HOLY WELL 1896 37469

independent, if not to say troublesome, line. In 1598, he was fined for keeping a greyhound bitch and for fighting John Grastie; in 1610, he was still keeping greyhounds, but he had also laid a net to poach fish in the Stanley moat, and a capon, stolen from Lady Stanley, was found in his house; in 1611, he had neglected to keep his ditches clear up on the Edge and he had been fighting again, this time with his brother, Thomas. The 1610 and 1611 Court leet records are full of such misdemeanours; the first Sir Thomas had died, his widow was running the manor for their young son and some villagers seem to have tried to take advantage of the situation. The Brynlow Hill area of Alderley does appear to have been the rough end of the village at the end of the 16th century. Not only is Randle Mottershead in trouble in 1598, his neighbour, Edward Oldham, from what is now Armstrong's Farm, was fined for gambling with his friends at bowls, and Thomas Deane of Brynlow had illegally burnt furze on the Edge.

Randle Mottershead's son, Robert, was in trouble in 1623 for burning furze on the Edge and in 1651 his grandson, Thomas, was fined for trespassing on Will Bradford's land. Interestingly, the Mottersheads' many infractions of the local laws do not stop them acting as jurors at the court; as one of the established farming families in the area they would have known the customary law, and their neighbours trusted their judgement in such matters. The 1684 terrier shows that Thomas's son, another Reginald, signing immediately after the gentry in the parish, had a surprisingly Italianate signature, suggesting he was well educated. The Mottersheads moved away to Fitton Town at the other end of Over Alderley in the early 18th century, but their old farm was known as Mottersheads until after Sir

**ALDERLEY EDGE, CASTLE ROCK c1955** A29014

Edward Stanley had a barn built there in about 1750. Whitewashed, its visibility as a landmark led the farm itself to be known as White Barn Farm and later to give its name to the road leading up to it.

This settled farming community, dominated by the Stanleys who owned most of the land in the township, was to remain unshaken until the estate was sold in 1938. However, that great revolution in Nether Alderley's history was to come after a far greater industrial and economic transformation that affected everyone in the area at the end of the 18th century.

CHAPTER FOUR

# CHANGES - THE IMPACT OF THE INDUSTRIAL REVOLUTION

UP to the end of the 17th century Wilmslow and Alderley had been fundamentally rural. There may have been a little medieval iron working on the slopes of Alderley Edge in the Middle Ages, and the old mineholes on the Edge were a well known part of the landscape, but that was all.

The mines on Alderley were the first industrial developments to change the situation. Up to the Civil War exploitation of strategic minerals such as copper was controlled by a Crown licensing system, but after 1660 mineral rights were firmly in the landowners' hands and they could think about exploiting them. The Stanleys let out their mineral rights to local businessmen. We know a little about these late 17th-century mines, not so much from any estate documents, but from the quarter sessions records after a riot at the mines in 1696.

Apparently there were two rival consortia, both claiming that they held a lease to mine from the Stanleys. One group of workmen decided to evict the other lot, in occupation down the mines, forcibly. They hauled the occupiers out by chains after the rope had been cut when it got round the neck of one of the men, John Thompson, and threatened to strangle him. Luckily he was not killed. The fracas came to the magistrates' notice, and after they had taken evidence from everyone all the men were bound over to keep the peace.

Prospecting for mining continued in the 18th century. One speculator, James Abbadine, built a smelter on the Edge in the early 18th century, but then failed to make a profit and had to abandon his enterprise. Around 1760, Charles Roe from Macclesfield took a lease to prospect for copper on the Edge. At one time he had up to 30 men working up there, but when Parys Mountain began to be opened up on Anglesey, Roe abandoned Alderley for the richer ores in Wales. As Dr Holland said in his survey of the economy of Cheshire in the early 19th century, everyone who looked for copper or lead on the Edge found evidence of its presence, but never enough to support a profitable business.

One mineral found on the Edge that caused great excitement when it was identified in 1805 was cobalt. This was the time of the French Wars, and because of the Napoleonic blockade Britain could not get her normal supply of this mineral from the continent. Cobalt had become an essential dye in the pottery and textile industry and British cobalt could command high prices at this time.

## Fact File

*Charles Roe had brass works in Macclesfield and near Bosley. He hoped Alderley copper would supply both foundries, and took a lease to prospect for copper on the Edge.*

## WIVES & DAUGHTERS

Some people think that Dr Holland of Knutsford was the model for Dr Gibson in Elizabeth Gaskell's novel 'Wives and Daughters'.

John Stanley thought he was going to make his fortune, and so did the miners, who, led by Thomas Ashton, built a steam engine and a windmill on the Edge to help process the ore along with the rest of the lead they were bringing out. John's wife, Maria, was more sceptical, and she was the one proved right, as once peace came, and normal supplies of cobalt from Europe were imported again, Alderley's cobalt mining ceased.

However, this stage in Alderley's history is still making its mark on the ground. The south side of the National Trust woods on the Edge is called Windmill Wood, and about 100 metres from the road down the public footpath is a bare patch of land where nothing has grown for 200 years. This is because of the contamination in the ground from all the lead that was crushed there.

Wilmslow was also developing its own industry; however here it was along traditional domestic lines, although with a new and exotic fibre, silk. First of all it was silk buttons, that essential accessory in gentlemen's fashion in the early and mid 18th century, when a coat could have upwards of a couple of dozen large, decorative buttons on it. Like much of industry in the early 18th century it was a rural rather than an urban occupation.

Then it was silk weaving. Silk was woven at home, the thread coming from the new doubling mills in Macclesfield, Stockport or from the silk mill in the Carrs by the Bollin. This silk mill was off Hawthorn Lane; it was a substantial four-storey building. Later, after the silk industry went into a decline, it was a fustian mill and then a laundry that boasted it returned everything to its customers except the dirt. However in the 18th century, when silk weaving was prosperous in East Cheshire, the children and women would wind the silk on to bobbins and the men wove the cloth. When the piece of silk was finished it was taken to or collected by the merchant and the family paid for its work.

This method of out-working had developed from the way the wool industry had been organised for centuries, where it could often be combined with subsistence farming. Here in Wilmslow it may have started like this, a way for a peasant family to supplement its income, and when button making was still the main business it provided work for the women in the household while the men got on with the farming. However, once weaving, a job done by the men in the family, became established then a silk-weaving family moved away from agriculture and depended entirely on the silk industry for its income.

One of the reasons for this was the high level of skill that was necessary to weave the fibre, especially after the Jacquard system of brocade weaving was introduced at the end of the 18th century. Silk weavers needed soft hands; calluses snagged the fibres and ruined the sheen of the finished material, so weavers could not combine their work at the loom with any form of hard outside labour that might harden their hands.

Consequently silk weaving became an urban or village occupation and the weavers tended to congregate together in distinctive forms of terrace housing. Two up, two down living accommodation and, at the top, to catch the best of the daylight, was the characteristic wide attic window of the weaving loft. There are few examples left in Wilmslow, but along the Manchester Road some can still be seen. One reason why these buildings survived the 19th-century development of the community was that silk weaving lasted as a hand-made domestic industry into the later 19th century, long after other fibres had gone into the mill to be processed; the early machine looms were too rough with the silk to produce an acceptable product.

Besides the silk mill in the Carrs that used the Bollin water to power its winding frames, there were other textile works in the town. A look at the trade directories of the early 19th century reveals small cotton mills, fustian works and other industries along the Bollin, taking advantage of its power. The relics of these have almost completely disappeared now, so it is difficult to see where they were. The Carrs themselves are now much valued amenity space for the whole of Wilmslow. They were saved from development when in 1925 they were given to the people of Wilmslow by Henry Boddington, who lived at Pownall Hall.

When Samuel Greg started the Styal cotton-spinning mill in 1784, it fitted into a typical late 18th-century industrial scenario. Now when we see the mill at Styal, beautifully preserved by the National Trust at the bottom of an attractive wooded valley, it appears to be isolated and almost unique (see page 66). However, Greg knew he could call on not just the fast-flowing river to give him the power he needed for his machinery, but also the textile-working expertise in the neighbourhood. Almost certainly he would have expected to recruit his weavers locally.

We have to go back to 1784 to see what Samuel Greg was doing. He came from a successful Lancashire/Ulster clothier background, able to draw on his family network for advice and support. His uncles, the Hydes, who were his partners in the early days, had already started a small water-powered cotton-spinning mill near Eyam in Derbyshire. However, by the late 18th century suitable water-power locations were becoming scarce to find and expensive to lease in Derbyshire, and the partners decided to look further afield. The Bollin, always a fast-flowing river, here runs even more quickly through a thickly wooded ravine. The natural fall in

**WILMSLOW, THE CARRS PLAQUE 2005** ZZZ05395 (Clare Pye)

The plaque on the entrance gate to the Carrs on Chancel Lane. Near here was Wilmslow's silk mill.

the water after the confluence of the Bollin and the Dean Water meant the mill could get its power without extensive engineering. Styal's location two miles or so downstream from Wilmslow out in open country meant that the incomers could not be accused of stealing other businesses' power by setting up too close to them; and the Earl of Stamford, keen to increase the value of his estates in a comparatively undeveloped area, was prepared to grant them a lease.

However, a spinning mill did need a concentration of labour at hand, and like many mill owners of the day Greg decided to use children's nimble fingers to piece

**Fact File**

*The Macclesfield area has the greatest concentration of urban weavers' cottages in the country.*

the threads and keep the machinery clean. The readiest source of children was pauper apprentices, and in 1793 the Apprentice House was built on land acquired again from the Stamfords. This use of apprentices was open to abuse, as the children's official guardian was their employer, the mill owner. He was also likely to be the local magistrate who was supposed to keep an eye on the welfare of pauper children in his area. The clash of interests is obvious.

However, compared to some of the other mill owners, the Gregs appear to have discharged their responsibilities fairly. The Greg women took an interest in the apprentices, organising classes to teach them to read on their Sunday off. Looking at the children's diet reveals they were eating no worse food than many other working class children of their day. Nearly all children from poor families at this time contributed to the family income as early as they could, often

**WILMSLOW, MANCHESTER ROAD, A WEAVERS' COTTAGE 2005** W103706k (Clare Pye)

One of the weavers' cottages on Manchester Road still has its wide window at the top of the house.

**WILMSLOW, MANCHESTER ROAD, WEAVERS' COTTAGES 2005** W103705k (Clare Pye)

**WILMSLOW, THE BOLLIN 2005** W103708k (Clare Pye)

Looking down the Bollin towards Styal.

**WILMSLOW, THE FOOTBRIDGE ON THE CARRS 2005**
W103707k (Clare Pye)

Walking the dog over a footbridge in the Carrs is part of many Wilmslow people's daily routine.

with scant attention being paid to any form of education beyond rudimentary literacy.

As the works at Styal expanded, so did the whole industrial estate. When Greg introduced power looms he needed to provide accommodation for adult workers as well as pauper apprentices, so the Styal Village was created, with its neat well-built dwellings, company shop, farm, chapels and school. Greg bought the freehold of the land from the Earl of Stamford so that he could have control over even more aspects of his workers' lives, including keeping an eye on how much they drank at the Ship Inn.

**WILMSLOW, CARRS PATH c1955** W103009

## THE EARLS OF STAMFORD

The Earls of Stamford owned the old Booth lands in Wilmslow, following the marriage of Mary Booth, heiress to the estate, to Harry Grey, 4th Earl of Stamford, earlier in the century. Thanks to the terms of her father's will and her marriage settlement, Mary, now Countess of Stamford, remained the active controller of her inheritance throughout her life. Her father had trained her in estate management so that she was able to do this.

STYAL, THE VILLAGE 1897 39617

Styal village, built by the Gregs for their workers in the early 19th century.

Like many industrialists at this time, Greg started out as a nonconformist, in his case, a Unitarian, and at Styal village is the Unitarian chapel he built, besides the Methodist chapel which he allowed his workers to convert from an old barn. However, as his memorial in St Bartholomew's suggests, rising prosperity, membership of the local bench and country living in general encouraged a move over to the established church, and the Greg family remained Church of England after his death in 1828.

Expanding the works meant increasing the power. A higher weir was built and the tail race extended, so that the water wheel was made larger and gave more power. The raising of the weir did affect the river upstream, and the old ford across the river to Pownall Hall became too deep and had to be replaced with a bridge. The long tailrace meant that the Gregs had to buy up land down the Bollin. This need to control the river for quite a long way either side of the mill explains the rather curious shape of the National Trust holding in the area. The wiggly purple boundary on a large scale map shows that the Trust needs to control the water of the Bollin just as much

## Fact File

*The earliest cottages in Styal village were barn conversions. Each cottage took up a bay of the large brick-built barn from the old farm.*

STYAL, THE UNITARIAN CHAPEL 1897 39618

Greg's Unitarian Chapel in Styal Village.

as the Gregs did. The appearance of the mill also tells a lot, in particular the big clock in the pediment of the oldest part of the mill. Once this clock ruled everything at Styal, clocking in and clocking out the workers, and all the cottages that had timepieces would set them according to the big clock at the mill.

It is during this third quarter of the 18th century that life began to change in the whole of the Wilmslow-Alderley area. The coming of large-scale manufacturing industry was one sign. However, the character of the area was going to change even more when the infrastructure was developed. Someone who left the area in 1770 and returned 20 years later would have found some profound alterations to the place.

The countryside would have looked a lot tidier, as many of the open uncultivated spaces grazed by the farmers' animals, the common land, had been enclosed. Only parts of Lindow Moss remained as they always had been; the peaty bog extending into a number of parishes resisted attempts to drain it and make it more profitable to the landowner. However, the Moss was once much larger than it is now. Lindow End on the Mobberley Road is a good mile from the present bog. One characteristic of the old moss can still be seen in the field pattern, long thin fields branching off an access right of way. These are 'moss rooms', individual holdings of peat bog now drained into pasture.

Alderley Edge was enclosed; the Stanley part in 1775 and the Trafford side a few years later. Both landowners decided the ground was too poor for cultivation and planted

WILMSLOW, CARRS BRIDGE c1955 W103008

STYAL, THE COTTON MILL 1897 39616

## SALTERSFORD HALL

Saltersford Hall in the middle of Lindow Moss gets its name from the packhorse trains that carried salt from the Cheshire wiches to Stockport and on to Derbyshire.

trees on the Edge. Many of the magnificent beech trees on the Edge date from this time, as do the clumps of Scots Pine. This tree was a favourite for poor land, 'Scots Pines are suited to Mancunian Mosses', said a tree expert of the day, and you can often identify late 18th- and early 19th-century attempts to develop old moss land and other poor soils by clumps of mature Scots pines. They can be found on Soss Moss, Sandle Heath and parts of Lindow Moss.

The Stanleys in particular were concerned to landscape their part of the Edge to fit in with the legend of Alderley Edge. This tells of a Mobberley farmer going over the Edge one late autumn morning to Macclesfield market to sell his white mare. An old man stops him and offers to buy the animal. When the farmer refuses, the old man says that he will be waiting for the farmer when he returns, as he knows he will not find a buyer at the market. So it happens, and when the farmer is stopped again in the evening on his way home, he agrees to sell his mare to the old man. He is told to follow and they walk over the Edge, eventually coming to a set of iron gates, which open at the old man's command to reveal a long passage going down into the hill. Now very frightened, the farmer follows the old man inside, and they eventually come to a great cavern full of 100 sleeping knights and 99 white mares. The old man tells the farmer to take as much gold as he wants for his horse and then to get out of the cave. Running out of the passage, the gates clang behind him and he is alone on the Edge to make his way back home. Never again was the farmer to find the iron gates, though he and many others since have searched for them.

### Fact File

*The old beech trees along the top of Artists Lane in Alderley are the survivors of a tree nursery established by the Stanleys in the middle of the 18th century.*

The original story had no Arthurian elements to it; these were added in the 19th century. However, under the Stanley auspices, a Druids' Circle was built on the Edge and the Miners' Arms became the Wizard Inn. Louisa Stanley also wrote a small book, 'Alderley Edge and its Neighbourhood', as a guide to the Edge. Being a lady, she published it anonymously, in 1843.

However, there had been even more changes in Alderley. In 1779, the Old Hall in Nether Alderley burnt down. The only part that was saved was the servants' quarters at the back. Sir John and Lady Stanley were travelling back from Chester when it happened and all

ALDERLEY EDGE, THE STONE TABLE OF THE WIZARD 1896 37466

The Druids' Circle, Alderley Edge.

they heard from Knutsford onwards was the dreadful news that their home was burning. Apparently the fire did not seem serious at first and the Stanley's steward, Mr Sherwood, forbade the emptying of the estate office. Suddenly the roof was alight and the molten lead flowing down meant that further salvage was impossible. The Stanleys arrived to be greeted by their housekeeper, 'Oh, my lady! Everything's gone! But we've saved the jam!' She had emptied her side of the house and saved not just the jam but the family receipt book as well, one of the few early Stanley records to survive the fire and now in the Cheshire Record Office.

The Stanleys did not attempt to repair their old home. Instead they moved into the Park House, the dower house in the south of the park. Sir John and his wife, Margaret Owen of Penrhos in Anglesey, spent much of their time away from Alderley, Margaret in her own house in Wales and Sir John, who was a Gentleman of the Bedchamber, in London. Consequently, when their son John married Maria Holroyd, in 1796, the Park House was free for the young couple to make it their home. They lived here until 1850, when John, now the 1st Lord Stanley, died at the age of 85. Such a long residence meant that this energetic and intelligent pair had a tremendous effect on Alderley and its people.

They were great improvers, John on the land, and Maria with the people. Almost as soon as John Stanley came to Alderley he began planting trees on the Edge and on Soss Moss, while Maria started a school for the girls of the parish on the site of the present Nether Alderley primary school. (The boys already had their own school in the churchyard at St Mary's.) She organised smallpox vaccinations and a soup kitchen when times were bad. Their daughter Louisa said that her parents combined the children's birthdays with the appropriate estate celebrations for the time of year. There were lots of these festivities as there were nine surviving Stanley children, a noisy and energetic family. Maria's much loved aunt said at one time that she regretted not seeing John and Maria at a family gathering, but eight little Stanleys would have been just too much.

**NETHER ALDERLEY, THE PLAQUE OVER THE SCHOOLHOUSE DOOR 2005** ZZZ05396 (Clare Pye)

**NETHER ALDERLEY, THE SCHOOL HOUSE 2005** N148708k (Clare Pye)

The 17th-century schoolhouse in St Mary's churchyard.

> **Fact File**
>
> *Margaret Owen of Penrhos in Anglesey, who married Sir John Stanley of Alderley, was very keen on the safety of sailors off Anglesey. She took part in rescuing shipwrecked sailors and was behind the building of the first South Stack lighthouse on the island.*

At first, the couple had four daughters in very quick succession and then twin sons, Edward and William. There was much celebration on the estate at the christening of the heir to the family, and 21 years later, the Stanleys built the Tenants' Hall specifically for the week-long series of parties that were held for the twins' joint coming of age. As John Stanley inherited extensive property in North Wales from his mother, it was decided as soon as the boys were born that William would have these lands and so not suffer from being born ten minutes after his brother.

> **Fact File**
>
> *In 1786, the elder Sir John Stanley gave his son John the income from Fernhill as part of his allowance when he came of age.*

One other great change had happened before John and Maria Stanley moved in. In 1780, only a year after the fire at the Old Hall in Alderley, a turnpike was built between Congleton and the bridge over the Bollin in Wilmslow. There it connected with the turnpike from Manchester that had been built a few years before. This road is, of course, the equivalent of the modern A34, the great north-south route connecting Manchester with the Midlands and the South. At last these previously quite isolated communities were connected to the outside road by a decent route.

> **Fact File**
>
> *After Maria Holroyd married John Stanley in 1796 her nicknames for her husband were 'The Man' and 'The Crow', the last because he had black hair and eyebrows.*

Originally in Wilmslow the turnpike came down Grove Street and past the church along Chancel Lane to cross the Bollin. It then had a steep climb up the banks of the Bollin along what is now Old Road. This hill was difficult for the horses to negotiate, and in 1834 a new, higher bridge was built 50 yards up the river, and the coaches now swung up Mill Street and then turned to go over the Bollin. The bridge was widened when the first Wilmslow bypass was built in the 1920s, but the original arch can be seen on its west side.

Turnpikes were financed by tolls paid by the traveller according to the assumed damage they were likely to do to the road. They were not popular with the locals. In particular, in Wilmslow, the tollgate out of the village was at the top of Grove Street, indeed this street, going straight down to the church, was built by the turnpike trustees and they charged accordingly. As Grove Street developed into Wilmslow's main street in the 19th century and the toll bar was still there in 1870, one can understand the community's annoyance. There were further tollgates along the road by the King's Arms, Street Lane Ends (the de Trafford) and Monksheath.

Down in Alderley, the route of the turnpike was altered in 1799 and again 20 years later, as the Stanleys extended their park and gained more privacy for the new house they had built in 1817-18 to replace the old Park House. Alderley also had its own set of problems for the trustees to solve. In the 1830s Hayman's Quarry had opened up on Finlow Hill, and at this time it was supplying stone to redevelop Capesthorne Hall. The heavy stone wagons came down Bradford Lane, turned left and had free use of the road until they reached Monksheath, which was very annoying for the trustees. They discussed various solutions, none of which were workable. Then about six months later, one of the trustees, William Davenport of Capesthorne offered, *ex gratia*, and with no strings attached, the sum of ten guineas to offset any damage the wagons may have caused. This money was happily accepted by his fellow trustees. Davenport had been present at the original discussion, but not a word did he say at the time, however one hears the clunk of heavy hints being thumpingly dropped.

**WILMSLOW, THE BOLLIN BRIDGE 2005**

W103709k (Clare Pye)

The A34 crosses the Bollin by the original turnpike bridge.

**WILMSLOW, THE BOLLIN BRIDGE 2005**

ZZZ05397 (Clare Pye)

The turnpike bridge was built in 1834.

One of the other trustees was the Reverend Edward Stanley, brother of the 1st Lord Stanley, who was Rector of Alderley for over 30 years before he became Bishop of Norwich. He was an outstanding man, a scholar and a scientist, energetic in his ministry, liberal in his views and practical in his philanthropy.

WILMSLOW, GROVE STREET 1897 39604

**WILMSLOW, GROVE STREET c1955** W103006

The top of Grove Street, Wilmslow, before Barclay's Bank moved from Bank Square to its present location.

**WILMSLOW, GROVE STREET 2005** W103710k (Clare Pye)

The turnpike toll bar was here. Looking at the elegant design of Barclay's Bank on the corner, it seems surprising that it was severely criticised when it was built 40 years ago.

His sister in law, Maria Stanley, was quite right when she said Edward was the best thing that had happened to Alderley for a long time. There are many tales about him. One was about the time he broke up a bare-knuckle fight among the miners on the Edge by sheer force of his personality and the respect he was held by everyone. Another told of the time when he was about to leave the parish for Norwich. He went round every parishioner' house to say goodbye, and when he rode into the rectory stable yard for the last time, his old black pony dropped dead and had to be buried in the garden.

One of his most visible legacies in the village is the extension he built on to the 17th century schoolhouse, now used as the parish rooms. His children were also distinguished, two of his sons exploring and mapping Australia and New Guinea. Owen Stanley's plotting of

ALDERLEY EDGE, THE VILLAGE SMITHY 1896 37477

The village smithy was in Bradford Lane. The lane was altered by the Stanleys 100 years before this photograph was taken.

In the garden of the old rectory in Nether Alderley is a huge scarlet rhododendron, reputedly planted in 1815 to commemorate the Battle of Waterloo, one of the earliest rhododendrons in the country.

the land and the coastal seas was so accurate that his charts were still being used by the Allies 100 years later when they were fighting the Japanese. The third son became Dean of Westminster and a confidante of Queen Victoria. Edward's daughter Mary was one of Florence Nightingale's nurses in the Crimea. She and her mother, Kitty, are buried under the old yew tree in St Mary's churchyard.

However, all of these changes were taking place in an essentially rural context; the old landowners were still dominant in the countryside and the social changes caused by the Industrial Revolution had not yet touched the area. All was to change with the next great development, the coming of the railways.

**NETHER ALDERLEY, THE SCHOOL ROOM, NOW THE PARISH HALL 2005** N148709k (Clare Pye)

This extension to the 17th-century schoolroom was built by the rector, Edward Stanley. It is now the parish hall.

**NETHER ALDERLEY, ST MARY'S CHURCHYARD, KITTY AND MARY STANLEY'S GRAVE 2005** N148710k (Clare Pye)

Kitty and Mary Stanley's grave beneath the ancient yew tree in St Mary's churchyard. Mary Stanley was one of Florence Nightingale's nurses in the Crimea.

**A SECTION OF A COUNTY MAP OF CHESHIRE SHOWING WILMSLOW AND SURROUNDING AREA c1850**

From Manchester
Matley
Godley
Mottram in Longdendale
Hyde
Hattersley
To Manchester
From Manchester
Brinnington
Wernith
Bredbury
Romily
Carrington
Ashton on Mersey
Sale
Partington
Carrington Moss
Canal
Northenden
STOCKPORT
Warburton
Cheadle Bulkeley
Timperley
Bridgewater's
Baguley
Etchells
Offerton
To Chapel en le Frith
Bramhall
Marple
Dunham Massey
ALTRINCHAM
Torkington
River Goyt
Peak Forest Canal
Agden
Bowdon
Cheadle Moseley
Bollington
Hale
Norbury
Millington
Riv. Bollin
Poynton
Distley
Ashley
Handforth with Boxden
Canal
Yeardsley
Worth
Rosthern
Riv. Birkin
Macclesfield
Whaley
Mere
Woodford
Pownal Fee
Bollen Fee
Lyme Handley
Tatton
Wilmslow
Newton
Kettleshulme
Mobberley
Adlington
Taxal
Tabley Superior
Fulshaw
Mottram St Andrew
Pott Shrigley
Chorley
Butley
Over Knutsford
KNUTSFORD
Great Warford
Prestbury
Martall
Bollington
Tabley Inferior
Bexton
Alderley Inferior
Alderley Superior
Tytherington
Rainow
Toft
Ollerton
Fallybroom
Plumbley
Little Warford
Upton
Hurdsfield
Macclesfield Forest
Little Peover
Birtles
Chelford
MACCLESFIELD
Lostock Gralam
Nether Peover
Peover Sup.r
Snelson
Capesthorne
Henbury
Hulse
Allostock
Old Withington
Pexall
Birches
Barnshaw
Lack Dennis
Rudheath
Blackden
Sutton
Stublach
Goostrey
Lt. Withington
Siddington
Gawsworth
Wildboar Clough
Byley with Yatehouse
Leese
Twemlow
Cranage
Marton
Ravenscroft
Kermincham
Riv. Dane
Swettenham
North Rode
Cotton
Church Hulme
Wincell
Sproston
Somerford Booths
Eaton
Bosley
To London
Kinderton
Davenport
Hulme Walfield
Mooresbarrow cum Parme
Brereton
Summerford
Radnor
Buglawton
Sutton
Hulme
Bradwell
Smethwick
Tetton
CONGLETON
Moston
Arclid
Astbury
To Leek
SANDBACH
Smallwood
Moreton
Elton
Grand
Aleumlow
Newbold Astbury
To Hanley
Wheelock
Beckton
Riv.

CHAPTER FIVE

# THE COMING OF THE RAILWAYS AND THE TRANSFORMATION OF WILMSLOW AND ALDERLEY

TRAFFORD ARMS HOTEL.

THE MODERN RAILWAY system started in the north-west with the opening of the Liverpool to Manchester line in 1830. Its success stimulated the first railway boom of the 1830s; businessmen were keen to speculate and this led to a rash of Railway Acts. One of the new companies, the Manchester and Birmingham Railway had a bill passed in 1837 permitting a railway to be built from Manchester, via Stockport to Wilmslow, and on to Stoke on Trent and Birmingham. They also proposed a branch line to Crewe with a junction in Chorley where the new railway would cross the old turnpike road. By the time that the railway was built the line to Stoke via Congleton had been abandoned, and the only line that was built was the line to Crewe via Holmes Chapel. The Manchester and Birmingham Railway Company later became part of the London and North Western Railway

The railway opened on 10 May 1842. However, the alterations to the original plan left the railway company with a seemingly superfluous station between Wilmslow and Chelford at Chorley. This is the genesis for the development of the first planned railway commuter village in the north-west, Alderley Edge village. As the railway opened, the company and the main landowner, Sir Humphrey de Trafford, were already negotiating for their mutual benefit. De Trafford agreed to release a number of 4- to 5-acre plots to developers, and the railway

ALDERLEY EDGE, THE RAILWAY STATION 1896 37446

Alderley Edge village railway station in 1896. In the background is the Queen's Hotel.

**ALDERLEY EDGE, THE WIZARD'S WELL c1955** A29016

The Wizard's Well, Alderley Edge. This well is a Victorian creation built to attract visitors to the Edge.

promised to build a hotel by the station, now Queens Buildings, and to provide certain inducements to encourage people to move to Alderley. The best known of these was a free first class rail pass between Alderley and Manchester for the head of any household living in a property worth more than £50 per year rateable value.

This was a considerable figure, and it meant that the developers intended to build sizeable villas for the mill owners and businessmen of Manchester. The development was in two main areas, around the station itself, especially down Brook Lane, and up the hill on the Edge. In the middle, between the London Road shops and the railway, was a development of two-up, two-down terraced housing for the workers who were to service the villas and their inhabitants. Later the east side of the London Road was developed for shopping, and more up-market terrace houses for the shopkeepers and other tradesmen were built in the streets between the main thoroughfare and Trafford Road.

**ALDERLEY EDGE, POST OFFICE SQUARE 2005**
A29705k (Clare Pye)

The 19th-century post office stands in front of the thatched roof of one of Alderley Edge village's original cottages, once the home of a de Trafford smallholder.

Mr Easted of the Manchester to Birmingham Railway Company had hoped to offer even greater inducements to the new inhabitants. He called on Lord Stanley in

Looking south down London Road, Alderley Edge village.

## DAY TRIPPERS

The first organised group of day-trippers to Alderley Edge was a Sunday school trip from Manchester. The children came out with their teachers and walked on the Edge very soon after the railway was opened in May 1842. According to the Stanleys, one of the coaches held buns for their tea.

1842 and tried to get him to agree to open the Wizard Woods on the Edge for an extra day for the exclusive use of the villa dwellers. The Stanleys, who already opened the woods to everyone for three days a week, would not budge; they saw no need to pander to the Cottentots, which was their name for the incomers. Indeed, they released very little of their own land for residential development until after 1900, despite their agent telling them it would be profitable.

The Stanleys greatly resented the railway company's annexation of the name Alderley Edge for the station, and the development of the new community under the name of Alderley Edge village. As far as they were concerned, Alderley was where they lived, a mile and a half to the south, Alderley Edge was the hill and the new village should really be called Chorley, as this was the name of the original township. When the 2nd Lord Stanley was Post Master General in the late 1850s, he gave instructions that letters for the new community, addressed as Alderley, should either be put in the dead letter box or be readdressed to Chorley. Such correspondence then often spent days sitting in the post office

**ALDERLEY EDGE, THE HOUGH 1896** 37464

The Hough below Alderley Edge in 1896. The swings are for the day-trippers who came out to the Edge on the railway.

**ALDERLEY EDGE, KEEPER'S COTTAGE 1896** 37479

Keeper's Cottage, now Beacon Lodge, Alderley Edge. Day trippers to the Stanleys' Wizard Woods beyond had to go through these gates.

ALDERLEY EDGE, TRAFFORD'S WELL c1955 A29019

Trafford's Well, Alderley Edge. This is round the corner from the Holy Well, and on Trafford, not Stanley land.

**Fact File**

*Alderley Edge parish church is dedicated to St Philip because it is a daughter church of St Bartholomew's in Wilmslow, and St Bartholomew baptised St Philip.*

in Chorley, Lancashire, before being sent down south. This was very annoying for the Manchester businessmen who now lived in the villas, and expected their mail to be quick and convenient.

However, the new community was a success. It had its own church, St Philip's, designed by Crowther, at first a chapel dependent on St Bartholomew's in Wilmslow, but later a parish church in its own right. There was a school beside it for the working families that were moving in, and a rather churchy looking Methodist chapel at the other end of the village. The shops developed and people moved in from outside to set up business. For instance, the local plumber, Walter Jaffrey, even moved down from Scotland in the early 1850s to establish himself and make money from the new villas and their owners.

**Fact File**

*Until Barclay's Bank was built in 1904, the Methodist Church in Alderley had the only outdoor clock in the village. It was adjusted to show the same time as the station clock.*

**ALDERLEY EDGE, THE CHURCH c1960** A29042

St Philip's Church, Alderley Edge village. The foreground is now the church car park.

**ALDERLEY EDGE, CHAPEL ROAD c1955** A29011

Looking along Chapel Road, Alderley Edge village, towards the spire of the Methodist church.

**ALDERLEY EDGE, FROM THE RAILWAY STATION 1896** 37445

The view of Alderley Edge village from the railway station towards the villas on the hill.

**ALDERLEY EDGE, LONDON ROAD c1965** A29047

Alderley Edge village's shopping street.

**Fact File**

*Three trains took commuters from Alderley into Manchester in the morning, the 7.30, 8.00 and 8.30. They were known as 'Striving, Thriving and Thriven'.*

Alderley Edge village was truly Victorian, a community of rigid social rules where class divisions remained strong until after the Second World War. Literally everyone knew their place as a person's address immediately told everyone where he or she fitted into the social pattern. 'The higher up the Hill, the richer the people' was the saying, 'and the slower they are to pay their bills', replied the tradesmen dependent on the villas. Down at the shops on the London Road, some catered for the villas, providing select goods to select people at select prices, and allowed the villa owners to set up accounts, others catered for the village and demanded cash on the nail. Those shops that sold to both ends of the market, such as Bilsboroughs, the ironmongers, had a differential price structure. The villa owners paid more if they wanted goods on account. In this way Mr Bilsborough hoped to offset the costs of waiting up to a year for the bill to be paid. Some people left tradesmen waiting a very long time. James Consterdine, the vicar, a model of Victorian respectability, ran up a personal jobbing bill at the vicarage with

ALDERLEY EDGE, THE DE TRAFFORD ARMS HOTEL 1896 37451

The de Trafford Arms Hotel, Alderley Edge village.

ALDERLEY EDGE, THE WESLEYAN CHAPEL INTERIOR 1896 37458

Walter Jaffrey the plumber for over £80 in six years in the 1860s. Perhaps Walter felt he could not put pressure on him as a bad word from the vicar might cause him to lose custom elsewhere.

Leisure was equally class-ridden. The Cricket and Tennis Club on Moss Lane was the exclusive domain of the villa families, shopkeepers and tradesmen frequented the Union Club in Steven Street and the working men used the local pubs, the de Trafford Arms, an especial haunt of the gardeners at lunchtime, the Royal Oak and the Drum and Monkey. The recently demolished Institute on the London Road was built to provide somewhere respectable and teetotal for the villa maids to spend their weekly free afternoons.

**Fact File**

*The one o'clock hooter at Masseys' the builders in Alderley was heard all over the village at lunchtime, and the gardeners drinking at the de Trafford Arms knew it was time to get back to work in the villa gardens.*

Even worship at church was divided; the villa owners went in the morning and the workers in the evening, a custom that started because the servants in the villas could not get to morning service as they were cooking their employers' Sunday lunch. Inevitably there was a social split between church and chapel, and two groups rarely socialised.

The Methodist Church in Chapel Lane was the main nonconformist place of worship in the new community. Others attended the Congregational Church, now the United Reformed Chapel, or the Friends' Meeting House in Wilmslow.

**WILMSLOW, THE FRIENDS' MEETING HOUSE 2005**
W103711k (Clare Pye)

This was the original Friends' Meeting House in Wilmslow.

There was quite a large Quaker community among the incomers. Prominent among them were the Satterthwaites, who started a dissenting academy known as the College. This had an enlightened curriculum, including both music and practical science lessons. The curriculum may have been forward looking, but otherwise the atmosphere must have been rather unpleasant, as Alderley's gas works were at the back of the College. One of its pupils, who later went on to become a master at the College, was the author George Gissing. The College has had a mixed history since the 19th century. Converted into flats after the Second World War, it lay empty for a while until it was recently converted into the Merlin pub. What teetotal Victorians would have thought of such a change can only be imagined.

Among the villa families, there were unwritten but strict codes of behaviour. If you had to ask what was the right thing to do, it was a sure sign that you were not socially acceptable. In particular there was a complicated etiquette over morning calls and calling cards. This was still going on after the Second World War. In 1948, one newly married woman can remember being called on by old Mrs Pownall, a great stickler, who left her card. Startled that the war had not ended such niceties, she had to rush out and get some cards of her own printed so that she could return the call in the approved manner.

With the coming of the railways Wilmslow also developed as a residential commuter community, although here the development was more mixed. Villas on the Alderley model were laid out in Fulshaw Park, which became a private gated residential development, rather like Victoria Park in Manchester, and other large villas were built in the area, but this was interspersed with less exclusive developments.

One of the reasons why development was more mixed was that the landowners did not have as firm a grip over the type of housing being built as they had in Alderley. It is worth looking at the attitude of the Earls of Stamford to their various estates in Cheshire.

WILMSLOW, THE CONGREGATIONAL CHURCH 1897 39610

The Stamfords had always been interested in maximising the value of their property. They had been ready to lease land to the Gregs in the 1780s and see a large scale mill built on their land, and at about the same time had even tried to develop Ashton under Lyme as a select Georgian planned town. When the railway came to Altrincham they had created the strictly controlled Stamford estate in Bowdon where the restrictions on the leases they granted made it clear they would not tolerate anything other than select residential use of the new houses, forbidding their use for trade or business.

**Fact File**

*There was a ban on the building of lunatic asylums on the Bowdon estate - one of the many restrictions imposed by the landowners.*

Oddly enough it was the new Bowdon bourgeoisie who were to play a part in the different character of the development of Wilmslow. The new inhabitants of Bowdon, having a distinct idea of their own worth and respectability, were shocked at the 7th Lord Stamford's choice of wife. Kitty Cox had been a circus equestrienne, and one of her brothers was a convicted criminal. They were disgusted at the idea that they would be expected to doff their hats to such a person, and forcibly stopped the local Grey tenantry from ringing the bells at Bowdon Church to celebrate the marriage. Nearly all the

WILMSLOW, STATION ROAD 1897 39606

respectable Cheshire society refused to have anything to do with Kitty. When the newly married couple attended Knutsford races every lady turned her back on them, and they were greeted by a sea of parasols and no faces. The Stamfords decided to leave Cheshire and rent out Dunham Massey.

They wanted to build a new house at Bradgate in Leicestershire and needed cash to pay for it. So the earl decided to sell most of his lands in the Wilmslow area. As he was leaving the neighbourhood, he was not particularly concerned with preserving the middle-class respectability of the area, and he was ready to maximise his short-term profit by selling the freehold of the land rather than continue to manage the estates through leasehold development. He was making it clear to Cheshire society that he was withdrawing from the county and did not intend to return. Even the sale was handled by the solicitors in Stourbridge who normally looked after his lands at Enville in Worcestershire, and the Altrincham estate office was made subservient to the Greys' main office in Ashton under Lyne.

The Gregs finally bought the freehold to all their land in the Styal area, and went on to build Norcliffe Hall for themselves so that they were no longer living right beside the mill. The other main purchaser of the Stamford land in Wilmslow was John Clarke Prescott. He did intend to develop the area for select residents and he set about the task immediately by demolishing the mill chimney from a small cotton mill that had previously dominated the village centre. If he wanted to appeal to the middle classes of Manchester, they needed no reminders of the industrial smoke and grime they

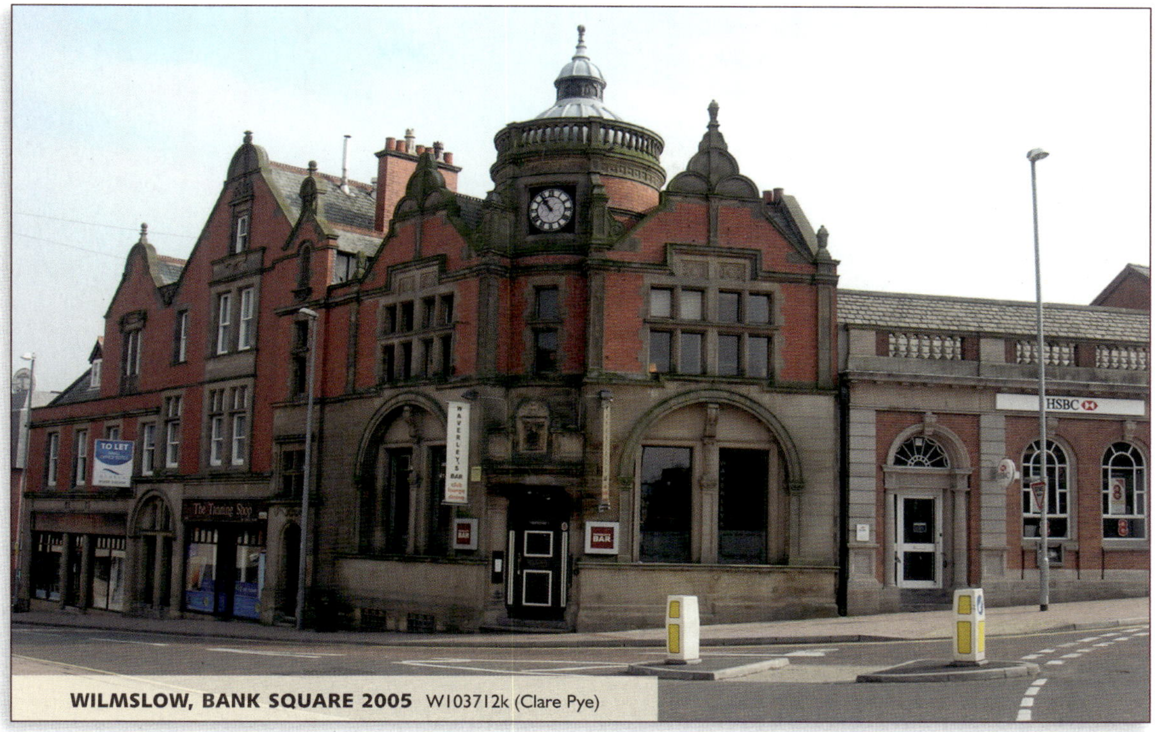


**WILMSLOW, BANK SQUARE 2005** W103712k (Clare Pye)

Now a bar, the brick building with cupola was once a bank that gave the square its name.

**WILMSLOW, LINDOW CHURCH 1897** 39620

St John's Church, Lindow.

were trying to leave behind them when they moved out to the countryside. However, compared to Alderley Edge village, the range of housing was more mixed. There was not such an unhealthy dependence of one social class on the other and more of the original community remained to remind everyone that Wilmslow was a much older and more diverse community.

One aspect of this mixed community can be seen in the persistence of unregulated individuals, often to be found in the vicinity of Lindow Moss, an area of land that still resisted improvement. After the Crimean War, the men who returned from the army were carrying a number of contagious diseases. They were made to camp out on the moss, so that they did not infect the town. Around 1900, a man with a dancing bear used to frequent Wilmslow. He bivouacked with his beast in a hollow on a sandy part of the moss, but was found dead one morning, apparently hugged to death by the bear. About this time Lindow also provided space for the local riflemen volunteers to practise. They are remembered in the place names Battery Lane and the Rifleman's Arms pub, and metal detectorists can still find bullets from their target practice.

More recently, at the start of the Second World War the local authorities commandeered part of the moss to set up

**WILMSLOW, LINDOW COMMON c1955** W103010

Lindow Moss, when peat cutting was still done by hand.

a permanent caravan site for Manchester's Gypsies, because they needed a permanent address for their ration cards. Not that they needed much in the way of rations; their poaching skills were legendary, and throughout the war the Plough and Flail was always able to sell a very good game pie to its customers, providing they did not ask too many questions. Even after the war Wilmslow people freely cut peat from the moss to supplement the coal ration, treating Lindow as an unregulated resource for the whole community.

Down south in Nether Alderley, where the Stanleys still controlled life, there were changes too, although the estate remained traditionally rural into the 20th century. Notably, from 1857-78, the Alderley Edge Mining Company dug for the copper and lead from the Edge. A new chemical extraction process, using hydrochloric acid to leach out the copper in the sandstone, made it possible to work the low ore-bearing sandstone profitably. Such was the technically advanced nature of the process that the Stanleys were proud to show their mines off to visitors. In the 1860s a Japanese delegation came, and the mines were lit up with magnesium flares in their honour.

The acid from this process created the Sandhills on Brynlow. Older people in the Alderley and Wilmslow area will remember playing on the Sandhills, especially in the 1940s and 50s, when trips to real sand at the seaside were few and far between. Even when the sand was cleared, the acid has created a peculiar ecological environment where the vegetation is remarkably different from the rest of the Edge.

To work these mines, the company needed expert workmen to lead the teams. Many of them came from the West Country, where they had hard rock mining experience in the Cornish tin mines. Most of these incomers only stayed a few years, but some, those who married local girls, settled permanently and their descendants are still here. However, the mines closed in 1878, when their lease from the Stanleys came up for renewal. Lord Stanley wanted more, the ore was getting harder to work, James Michell, the Mines Captain, had recently been killed in an accident and the steam engine had just blown up, so the company decided to call it a day. Later, at the time of the First World War, the then high price of copper encouraged a new company to start up again, but once the war was over, and prices returned to normal, the mines closed for a final time and in 1923 the equipment was sold off.

The Alderley Edge Mining Company was also responsible for creating the miles of underground passages beneath the Edge. There are almost as many paths below ground as on the surface. The miners also made the great opencast mining scar at Engine Vein. After the mines were officially closed, these tunnels became an irresistible temptation for the foolhardy to explore, sometimes at the cost of their lives. From the 1920s to the 1960s no Bank Holiday seemed to go by without the emergency services being called out to rescue someone who had got into difficulties down the mines. Public concern at these accidents led the authorities to try and make the Edge safer. Blocking up the mines only led to explorers breaking in; in one instance a new brick wall across West Mine was breached the following week by a grenade explosion. In the 1960s the opencast ravine leading to West Mine was filled in with household refuse, and the famous demolition expert Blaster Bates attempted unsuccessfully to blow up access to Engine Vein. The latter mine was made much safer in the early 1980s, when the Trust had a false floor constructed half way down. Now what appears to be the first cavern in Engine Vein is roofed by this concrete shelf, as it is really the bottom of the opencast part of the mine.

The mines are now in the care of the Derbyshire Caving Club. They have sealed off the entrances and make the ground above safe for visitors to the Edge, and they hold open days twice a year, when the public can enter the upper reaches of some of the mines. They will also take guided parties down by arrangement. When the mines are not open, those interested can see what they are like if they visit the small club museum at the Wizard Inn.

The copper mines were not the only odd feature of life in Alderley at the end of the 19th century. The 3rd Lord Stanley converted to Islam, and when he inherited the estate, he closed the public houses on his land. The Eagle and Child opposite the mill in Nether Alderley became a private house, the Iron Gates at Monksheath a farm, and the Wizard a tearoom for the walkers on the Edge. Although the latter has become a restaurant it still has a restricted licence. The Muslim Lord Stanley is buried apart from the rest of his family, in a small wood beside the A34 opposite the park.

ALDERLEY EDGE, WEST MINE 1896 37480

ALDERLEY EDGE, THE WIZARD INN 1896 37452

Once the Miners' Arms, this became The Wizard Inn in 1843.

**Fact File**

*When the Muslim 3rd Lord Stanley was buried, one of the younger members of the family was unsure how he should show respect. He doffed his hat, only for his Uncle Algernon to turn to him and say, 'Not your hat, boy, your boots!'*

When the Eagle and Child closed as an inn, it occasioned another change in Alderley life. For centuries, the Alderley Wakes had been held there beside the churchyard. This had been a truly village occasion, one which the Stanleys attended but did not control. All the local farming families tried to get back to Alderley for Wakes week in the third week of August. It always started in church, but apparently few people paid much attention to the religious service; they were too busy checking out their neighbours. Afterwards the inn served frumenty and beer and there was dancing on into dark.

After the Eagle and Child was closed the Wakes were still held, but up at the Wizard, and it became a teetotal occasion. There was still a religious element, as the day started with a service for the Alderley Oddfellows at St Mary's, after which they paraded up the hill to the Wizard, where there was a mixture of entertainment, including races, donkey rides, balloon ascents, brass bands and teas. After the First World War the date of the Alderley Wakes changed to Easter, but the fun still went on until 1939, with the fair set up in the field opposite the Wizard.

## Fact File

*The donkeys used in the Alderley Wakes were normally hobbled and allowed to graze on the Sandhills, only they broke free and invaded the gardens of the Hagg Cottages and ate the flowers.*

Wilmslow too had its Wakes, again an old custom dating from the Middle Ages. They took place in the first week of September, and stalls were set up between St Bartholomew's and the George and Dragon. Here there was no reforming landlord to spoil the fun, but, as the 19th century went on and Wilmslow grew as a dormitory town, new festivities were added to it, and the Wakes started to become known as the carnival. There was much competition, both privately and between businesses over the floats that paraded through the town. By the early 20th century the carnival's main purpose was to raise money for local hospitals and other charities, and everyone in the community joined in and enjoyed themselves.

Alderley Edge village too had its carnival, with a parade of floats, Sunday school children, friendly societies and church bands. Traditionally, those walking beside the floats had open umbrellas for people to throw in their contributions to help the Cottage Hospital.

There was also the Alderley Edge and Wilmslow Flower Society show, started in 1895. Many of the villas had splendid gardens,

ALDERLEY EDGE, THE COTTAGE HOSPITAL c1955 A29002

## OBADIAH BARBER

One year Obadiah Barber, who played the horse in the mummers' play, ran off with the money they had collected and spent it all on drink. Obadiah lived up at the Cuckoo's Nest, but later took to living rough in the woods.

and the rivalry was as much between the gardeners as the villa owners. At the end of the show a service was held in St Philip's and great tall bunches of delphiniums stood beside the pews. One person who can remember this says they reminded her of tall blue soldiers marching down the aisle.

In Nether Alderley, another custom continued that was peculiar to the estate, the Alderley Mummers. The village had a traditional Christmas mummers' play that was only performed for the Stanleys and their tenants in the Tenants' Hall at Alderley Park. As Kate Stanley said in the 1860s, other villages in the area had their Soulers, men who went round at All Souls' tide with a horse's head and a song, but in this district only Alderley had a play. It was also unique in that the play was the property of one extended family, the Barbers of Brynlow. They played all the parts. The mummers' play ceased its traditional character with the sale of the estate, but in the last few years it has been enthusiastically revived, no longer the exclusive property of one family, and it is performed round some of the local pubs in the area. Christmas cheer and mumming are still going strong.

Many of these traditional festivities came to an end in 1939, and after the war was over they were not always revived. One reason for this was that, with the coming of the Welfare State, local communities did not have to raise the money to fund their local hospitals directly. While it is right that such essential services no longer have to depend on charity for their survival, the loss of communal effort, pride and fun was greatly missed. Recently, with the revival of the Wilmslow Show, there have been attempts to bring some of this communal celebration back to the town

One festivity that has survived from before the war, and indeed goes from strength to strength, is the Alderley Edge Music Festival. Founded by Philip Godlee, who lived in Ryleys Lane and was the chairman of the Hallé Orchestra in the 1920s, it has its own Festival Hall. The music festival itself is run by a redoubtable team of volunteers and seems to involve everyone, not just individual musicians, but schools and other groups, and has for many years outgrown its original premises and now takes place in almost all the available space in the village.

## Fact File

*When Philip Godlee, chairman of the Hallé Orchestra, returned to work after a serious operation, the men with whom he usually shared the train compartment organised a celebration, a red carpet bordered with tubs of shrubs across the platform to the compartment door, and half a dozen Hallé brass players to sound a fanfare.*

In the weeks outside the festival in May, the Festival Hall now functions as the village hall for everyone in Alderley Edge village. The parish council meets here, Cheshire's branch of the Family History Society have their offices at the back, and many other village societies consider it their home. It has a superb sprung floor and during the Second World War functioned as a dance hall and a cinema. It was then known as the Regal, a favourite rendezvous for the American soldiers billeted in the village.

**WILMSLOW, THE WAR MEMORIAL 2005**
W103713k (Clare Pye)

Wilmslow's war memorial has more casualties for the First World War, but the plaque for the Second World War gives more details.

Both World Wars saw great changes in the area. In the First World War there was a prisoner of war camp at Handforth, so Wilmslow must have seen files of enemy prisoners marching through the community. More lasting in its impact was the sight of local men going the other way, out to fight, many of them never to return home. They are remembered on the local war memorials in the area. In both Wilmslow and Alderley Edge the memorials are sited by the parish church.

Perhaps Alderley's is the more poignant. When St Philip's was built it was a daughter church to St Bartholomew's, and from the start there was no graveyard round the building. Early settlers in the village were

**WILMSLOW, THE SECOND WORLD WAR MEMORIAL 2005** W103714k (Clare Pye)

The plaque for Wilmslow's dead of the Second World War.

WILMSLOW, THE MEMORIAL GARDENS c1955 W103003

ALDERLEY EDGE, RYLEYS LANE c1955 A29009

Alderley Edge's war memorial in Ryleys Lane, beside St Philip's Parish Church.

buried in Wilmslow. Later, when St Philip's became a separate parish, it was decided to create an interdenominational cemetery for everyone in the community and Lord Stanley donated some land on the Chelford Road for this purpose. However, the war memorial is beside the parish church. It is also on the corner of School Lane, down which many of the men would have gone to school, and opposite one of the entrances to the station, from which they would have departed for the last time. Indeed, if the station were not there nor would the village, so, in the true sense, Alderley's war memorial is at the heart of the community. The men are listed alphabetically, villa and village together.

In Nether Alderley, the memorial lists not only the men who were killed, but also the men who served, and did come back, a reminder of how almost all that generation of young men were swept up into the conflict. Some of the men who came back were wounded, and were nursed in the community. The Tenants' Hall at Alderley Park was used by the Manchester Regiment to convalesce after Gallipoli. In Alderley Edge village Brookdale was taken over by the Red Cross, and used as a centre for voluntary activity as well as a hospital. The matron was Emily Hutton. She received an OBE for her services after the War, but she never lived to collect it. Exhausted from her work, she succumbed to the Spanish flu epidemic in 1919, as much a victim of the war as the men she nursed.

## EMILY HUTTON

The people of Alderley Edge village clearly thought hospital matron Emily Hutton was a victim of the First World War, even though she died of flu in 1919, as her name is on the war memorial, separately inscribed at the base of the cross.

**ALDERLEY EDGE, DUKE STREET c1960** A29030

Duke Street, Alderley Edge village, looking towards the Edge and its villas.

Superficially, in the 1920s and 30s life in the villas in Alderley continued much as it had done before the war. There were still plenty of servants to run the big houses, and the social set-up remained as deferential as it had ever been. In Wilmslow, there was a rapid expansion of residential development, as the areas round Hawthorn and Pownall Halls were built up. These were solid detached houses in substantial gardens, perhaps not as grand as the 19th-century villas built 70 years before, but much more convenient for modern living and the smaller families that were common by then.

**THE REX 2005** W103715k (Clare Pye)

The Rex is a fine example of Art Deco architecture, but Wilmslow no longer has a cinema.

## Fact File

*Swiss Hill was used to test world-beating motor cars as the Railton family developed cars for Sir John Cobb in the 1930s, and tested hill starts up Swiss Hill.*

The road system was also modernised. Grove Street had developed in the late 19th century as Wilmslow's main shopping street, and it could no longer take the increased traffic that came with the development of the motor car. So Wilmslow's first by-pass was built to the east, and a new shopping parade was erected along its service road, including Wilmslow's smart new Art Deco cinema, the Rex. Reputedly, in the 1930s Oswald Mosley tried to use the steps of the Rex to inspect a march-past of his blackshirts. However, it was a dismal failure, as Wilmslow was clearly unreceptive to fascist ideas.

While it might be argued that between the wars Alderley Edge village and Wilmslow continued along the lines that had been set in the 19th century, the same cannot be said of Nether Alderley, where the old semi-feudal structure of the Stanley estate came to an abrupt end in 1938. Taxes and death duties were causing great problems for all the landed gentry at this time. In 1925 Lyulph, the 4th Lord Stanley, died: and less than six years later his son, the 5th Lord, died too. The 6th Lord Stanley, who was only 23, was faced with

## HAZELWOOD

Hazelwood, a house in Alderley Edge village, hides a fascist past. Apparently, underneath the carpet in the hall is a mosaic floor with Italian fascist symbols on it. It is now kept well covered up.

having to find two lots of death duties. He was not, by temperament, the man for such a task. 'He drank, he womanised and he gambled, and he was no good at any of it,' is the assessment of his cousin, the present Lord Stanley.

**ALDERLEY EDGE, THE TEA ROOM 2005**

A29707k (Clare Pye)

On the Edge, behind the Wizard Inn, is the tearoom, the National Trust Information Centre and the Derbyshire Caving Club Museum.

Such habits are expensive, and in 1938 he faced a crisis when his first wife, no longer prepared to tolerate his unreliable ways, left him and demanded a divorce. Without telling anyone in Cheshire the 6th Lord Stanley sold the whole estate to property developers. The first the estate knew about it was when the developers put the estate up to auction for residential development. It was a tremendous shock for everyone, something that elderly people in Alderley still remember as a real crisis.

The auction, which was held in Macclesfield in October 1938, was a spectacular failure, so much so that less than a tenth of the lots were sold. Inspection of the sale catalogues belonging to the people who were at the auction shows bids creeping up and then the lot being withdrawn as it had not reached the reserve price. The developers had created building plots of an acre each all over the Edge, but the farmers were not ready to pay developers' prices for their land, and the general gloom at the sale seems to have affected many other potential bidders. Anyway, October 1938, the time of the Munich crisis, was not a good time for people to go in for speculation.

**Fact File**

*After the failure of the estate auction in 1938 there was a second sale in Crewe in the spring of 1939, when most of the farmers bought their land. The prices were much lower, and later the development company went bankrupt.*

The failure of the sale did have one good result, as the Edge was saved from residential ribbon development. Dorothy and Margaret Pilkington, who lived at Firwood in Alderley Edge village, managed to get the Wizard Woods protected. They bought some of the land themselves and persuaded the County Council to buy more. After the Second World War had finished, the land was handed over to the National Trust so that they could preserve this open space for everyone to enjoy. Thanks to the Trust, the Edge is now better cared for and understood than ever before and they have proved worthy successor custodians to the Stanleys.

Alderley Park itself, where the house itself had largely burned down in 1932, was bought by ICI after the war. They set up their

**ALDERLEY EDGE, THE PILKINGTON FAMILY MEMORIAL 2005** A29706k (Clare Pye)

The memorial to the Pilkington family, who did so much to save Alderley Edge from development and made sure the National Trust was able to take it over.

pharmaceutical research laboratories in the Park. Now Astra Zeneca, it can also be argued that the company has taken over from the old landed gentry, at least in terms of employing local people and influencing the economic development of the whole area.

However, the Stanley sale removed the infrastructure from the estate and with it the support system for the tenants. Although most of the farmers were able to use government help to purchase their own farms, many of the cottagers and labouring families could not afford to buy their own homes. These cottages were inevitably bought up by incomers, who could afford to modernise them. Now, with the downturn in agricultural fortunes in the last decade, many of the farms are going the same way. Superficially, the countryside may look very much as it always has done, but a closer look reveals fundamental changes. One or two farmers now control most of the farming in the Nether Alderley area, and the old farmhouses have been sold off, perhaps with a few acres of amenity land for a child's pony, and the barns converted into houses.

**ALDERLEY EDGE, THE ENTRANCE TO THE ASTRA ZENECA LABORATORIES 2005** A29708k (Clare Pye)

The entrance to the present site of Astra Zeneca's laboratories goes past the old Stanley lodge into the park.

CHAPTER SIX

# ALDERLEY AND WILMSLOW TODAY

NOW, as we come into the third millennium, it is possible to see that all three communities have become essentially suburban areas, in that few people depend for their living on locally owned farms or industry. The service sector, in all its myriad forms, provides the majority of people with their livelihoods, and most of them look to Manchester or even further afield for the crucial decisions that shape their lives.

The area has also become almost entirely middle class and middle aged. With the rise in house prices and the sale of council houses in the late 20th century, working people and young couples looking for a place to start a family can find it very difficult to get anywhere to live in the area. Even the old terrace houses have been converted into bijou residences for the professional classes. This homogenisation of society means that the area has lost the variety of human inter-reaction that used to be there.

ALDERLEY EDGE, THE HIGH SCHOOL 1896 37454

Later the school became known as St Hilary's School

ALDERLEY EDGE, ST HILARY'S PARK 2005 A29709k (Clare Pye)

The original villa, Westwood, is just visible on the extreme right of the St Hilary's Park development. The development is named after St Hilary's School, now amalgamated with Mount Carmel School to form Alderley Edge School for Girls.

**ALDERLEY EDGE, A NEW ESTATE c1955** A29001

Council housing near the Circuit.

**ALDERLEY EDGE, WILTON CRESCENT c1965** A29045

Soon after the houses were built Wilton Crescent looked rather bleak, but the gardens have grown and in 2004 the residents of the Crescent celebrated 40 years of the estate.

**WILMSLOW, PARK ROAD 2005**

W103722k (Clare Pye)

Originally workers' cottages, the houses in Park Road have been smartened up and sold to young professionals.

One casualty of the increasing maturity of the population can be seen in Wilmslow Opera's recent problems. It is extremely difficult for them to raise a young enough chorus line to undertake such shows as 'The Mikado'. Make-up is not enough to convince an audience of the youthful innocence of three little maids when they are played by a trio of stalwart grandmothers.

Another aspect of the character of Wilmslow and Alderley Edge village may also be under threat. Both communities were known for the importance and character of their shopping centres, with a strong emphasis on family-owned businesses. Any stroll down Alderley's London Road today will now see premises boarded up, old buildings demolished and replaced by yet another apartment development. A shop goes and is replaced with another wine bar or bistro. It is significant that when one of these new apartment blocks was displaying its show home, the developers furnished it with a swanky kitchen, all steel and granite with every modern appliance on display, but no dining table. They expected potential purchasers to go out to eat.

Some quirky establishments are still going strong. Weinholt's is an Alderley institution. Interestingly, the bakers and confectioners discovered in the winter of discontent in the 1970s that they made as much profit being open for three days a week as they had when open six. Consequently, when the economic crisis eased, they continued to open just for the end of the week, a practice that still goes on.

**ALDERLEY EDGE, WEINHOLT'S 2005** A29712k (Clare Pye)

Weinholt's, bakers and confectioners, are shown here closed as ever, early in the week.

One facility the new eating places have embraced with enthusiasm is pavement tables. This is because of a property quirk in London Road. When the street was laid out in the 19th century, the buildings had small gardens in front of them. These went when the road and the pavements were widened, but the shops, not the council, own the few feet in front of their premises and so are able to put up tables, signs or whatever they want to help their business.

Grove and Water Street in Wilmslow are showing similar signs of retail degeneration.

**ALDERLEY EDGE, THE BRAZ 2005** A29711k (Clare Pye)

'The Braz' or Brazingamen's Bar, presumably a corruption of Alan Garner's novel 'The Weirdstone of Brisingamen', stands in front of Queen's Buildings, once a select family hotel.

**WILMSLOW, BANK SQUARE GARDENS c1955** W103007

Bank Square Gardens in 1955, before Barclays' Bank moved to the top of Grove Street.

**WILMSLOW, THE BYPASS 2005** W103716k (Clare Pye)

The Wilmslow bypass. Road and rail together emphasise Wilmslow's role as a commuter town.

Everyone blames the new bypass and the out of town shopping developments along it with their free parking. There would have been no Wilmslow bypass relieving the town of the worst of heavy through traffic without these retail companies putting up some of the money, so it looks as if there cannot be any improvement without pain.

Alderley Edge village is still without a bypass, although it has been planned since before the Second World War. Plans are made, displayed and public enquiries are held to argue over the merits of the details of the route, and then the proposal is shunted once again down the government's list of priorities. Meanwhile, Alderley Edge village suffers near gridlock almost every morning and evening as commuters to Astra Zeneca and Manchester, heavy trucks and parents on the school run all compete with parked cars along a road planned in the 1780s.

However, there is still much to celebrate in all the communities. Nether Alderley's pride in its parish church is self-evident. In 2000, to commemorate the 700th anniversary of the creation of the parish, the people here managed to re-hang the bells on a new steel

WILMSLOW, ROMANY'S CARAVAN c1955 W103001

'Romany' was the Rev George Bromwell Evens, famous for his wartime nature talks on radio's 'Children's Hour'. Romany's caravan is now sited next to Wilmslow Library. His dog, Raq, is buried beside the caravan.

frame, to restore the Stanley Pew completely to its Jacobean glory and to refurbish the coats of arms on the organ gallery at the west end of the church This was all done out of their own resources and with no help from the Lottery or other such government funds.

The continuing popularity of the Alderley Edge Music Festival, another success due entirely to the vigour and enterprise of local volunteers, has already been mentioned. In Wilmslow, the success of the Wilmslow Guild continues to grow and to spread its influence outside the confines of the town. The Guild in Bourne Street, behind the meeting room of the Society of Friends and founded in 1923, is a typical example of Quaker enthusiasm for self-directed self improvement. The residents of Bourne Street and Windsor Avenue may bemoan the students' parking habits on popular nights when fervent gardeners, bridge players and naturalists come together to pursue their hobbies. However, the Guild's determination to remain independent and give the people of Wilmslow what they want rather than what the powers that be think they ought to have can only be admired.

In other ways the practical philanthropy that is a mark of Wilmslow and Alderley life continues. In the 19th century, it may have been interest in hospital committees or charities in the Manchester slums. Individual families were known for their commitment to good causes. There had been the Moxons of Westbank in Alderley who held parties for the children of Moss Side and Hulme in their gardens, Miss Moxon taking in evacuees by the houseful during the Second World War. There was Margaret Pilkington, honorary director of the Whitworth Art Gallery, who oversaw its transfer to the University of

**WILMSLOW, THE ENTRANCE TO THE WILMSLOW GUILD, BOURNE STREET 2005** W103717k (Clare Pye)

Manchester after the reduction in value of its initial endowment made it impossible to continue as an independent concern.

Recently another charity founded in Wilmslow has become international in its scope. This is Wilmslow Wells for Africa. Set up by Wilmslow's churches, by concentrating on the basics of providing fresh, drinkable water to African villages, it is a prime example of Wilmslow's tendency to go for practical, often small-scale but truly life-transforming improvements in peoples' lives. It goes about its work in an unflashy but productive manner.

It would appear, then, looking at the development of these three communities, Nether Alderley, Alderley Edge village and Wilmslow, that the mottos of both one-time landowners in the area are still valid. 'Sans Changer', said the Stanleys. Much has changed in the area, particularly for the Stanley family itself, who have gone from their park for nearly 70 years, but much remains, particularly in the memories of local people and the landscape they inhabit. The de Trafford motto, 'Now Thus', however, appears more pragmatic and farseeing, ready to accept the inevitability of evolution and development, and to accept that each generation will mould the environment to its own needs, but never without taking into account the legacy of previous people who lived here.

**WILMSLOW, THE LEISURE CENTRE 2005** W103718k (Clare Pye)

Wilmslow's leisure centre, built in the old rectory's paddock, is always a busy place.

ALDERLEY EDGE FROM THE AIR 1964 AFA142211

# Francis Frith
## Pioneer Victorian Photographer

Francis Frith, founder of the world-famous photographic archive, was a complex and multi-talented man. A devout Quaker and a highly successful Victorian businessman, he was philosophical by nature and pioneering in outlook. By 1855 he had already established a wholesale grocery business in Liverpool, and sold it for the astonishing sum of £200,000, which is the equivalent today of over £15,000,000. Now in his thirties, and captivated by the new science of photography, Frith set out on a series of pioneering journeys up the Nile and to the Near East.

He was the first photographer to venture beyond the sixth cataract of the Nile. Africa was still the mysterious 'Dark Continent', and Stanley and Livingstone's historic meeting was a decade into the future. The conditions for picture taking confound belief. He laboured for hours in his wicker dark-room in the sweltering heat of the desert, while the volatile chemicals fizzed dangerously in their trays. Back in London he exhibited his photographs and was 'rapturously cheered' by members of the Royal Society. His reputation as a photographer was made overnight.

By the 1870s the railways had threaded their way across the country, and Bank Holidays and half-day Saturdays had been made obligatory by Act of Parliament. All of a sudden the working man and his family were able to enjoy days out, take holidays, and see a little more of the world.

With typical business acumen, Francis Frith foresaw that these new tourists would enjoy having souvenirs to commemorate their days out. For the next thirty years he travelled the country by train and by pony and trap, producing fine photographs of seaside resorts and beauty spots that were keenly bought by millions of Victorians. These prints were painstakingly pasted into family albums and pored over during the dark nights of winter, rekindling precious memories of summer excursions. Frith's studio was soon supplying retail shops all over the country, and by 1890 F Frith & Co had become the greatest specialist photographic publishing company in the world, with over 2,000 sales outlets, and pioneered the picture postcard.

Francis Frith had died in 1898 at his villa in Cannes, his great project still growing. By 1970 the archive he created contained over a third of a million pictures showing 7,000 British towns and villages.

Frith's legacy to us today is of immense significance and value, for the magnificent archive of evocative photographs he created provides a unique record of change in the cities, towns and villages throughout Britain over a century and more. Frith and his fellow studio photographers revisited locations many times down the years to update their views, compiling for us an enthralling and colourful pageant of British life and character.

We are fortunate that Frith was dedicated to recording the minutiae of everyday life. For it is this sheer wealth of visual data, the painstaking chronicle of changes in dress, transport, street layouts, buildings, housing and landscape that captivates us so much today, offering us a powerful link with the past and with the lives of our ancestors.

Computers have now made it possible for Frith's many thousands of images to be accessed almost instantly. The archive offers every one of us an opportunity to examine the places where we and our families have lived and worked down the years. Its images, depicting our shared past, are now bringing pleasure and enlightenment to millions around the world a century and more after his death. For further information visit: www.francisfrith.co.uk

# FREE PRINT OF YOUR CHOICE

**Mounted Print**

*Overall size 14 x 11 inches (355 x 280mm)*

**Choose any Frith photograph in this book. Please note: photographs with a reference number starting with a "Z" are not Frith photographs and cannot be supplied under this offer.**

Simply complete the Voucher opposite and return it with your remittance for £2.25 (to cover postage and handling) and we will print the photograph of your choice in SEPIA (size 11 x 8 inches) and supply it in a cream mount with a burgundy rule line (overall size 14 x 11 inches).

**Offer valid for delivery to one UK address only**.

***PLUS:* Order additional Mounted Prints at HALF PRICE - £7.49 each** (normally £14.99)

If you would like to order more Frith prints from this book, possibly as gifts for friends and family, you can buy them at half price (with no additional postage and handling costs).

***PLUS:* Have your Mounted Prints framed**

For an extra £14.95 per print you can have your mounted print(s) framed in an elegant polished wood and gilt moulding, overall size 16 x 13 inches (no additional postage and handling required).

**IMPORTANT!**

**These special prices are only available if you use this form to order. You must use the ORIGINAL VOUCHER on this page (no copies permitted). We can only despatch to one UK address. This offer cannot be combined with any other offer.**

*Send completed Voucher form to:*

**The Francis Frith Collection, Frith's Barn, Teffont, Salisbury, Wiltshire SP3 5QP**

# CHOOSE A PHOTOGRAPH FROM THIS BOOK

*Please do not photocopy this voucher. Only the original is valid, so please fill it in, cut it out and return it to us with your order.*

| Picture ref no | Page no | Qty | Mounted @ £7.49 | Framed + £14.95 | Total Cost £ |
|---|---|---|---|---|---|
| | | 1 | Free of charge* | £ | £ |
| | | | £7.49 | £ | £ |
| | | | £7.49 | £ | £ |
| | | | £7.49 | £ | £ |
| | | | £7.49 | £ | £ |
| | | | £7.49 | £ | £ |
| | | | * Post & handling | | £2.25 |
| | | | Total Order Cost | | £ |

*Please allow 28 days for delivery.*
*Offer available to one UK address only*

Title of this book ..............................

I enclose a cheque/postal order for £ ...........

made payable to 'The Francis Frith Collection'

OR please debit my Mastercard / Visa / Maestro card, details below

Card Number

Issue No (Maestro only) Valid from (Maestro)

Expires Signature

Name Mr/Mrs/Ms ..........................................

Address ..........................................

..........................................

..........................................

.......................... Postcode ......................

Daytime Tel No ..........................................

Email ..........................................

ISBN: 1-84589-222-4 Valid to 31/12/08

FREE PRINT - SEE OVERLEAF

## CAN YOU HELP US WITH INFORMATION ABOUT ANY OF THE FRITH PHOTOGRAPHS IN THIS BOOK?

We are gradually compiling an historical record for each of the photographs in the Frith archive. It is always fascinating to find out the names of the people shown in the pictures, as well as insights into the shops, buildings and other features depicted.

If you recognize anyone in the photographs in this book, or if you have information not already included in the author's caption, do let us know. We would love to hear from you, and will try to publish it in future books or articles.

## OUR PRODUCTION TEAM

Frith books are produced by a small dedicated team at offices in the converted Grade II listed 18th-century barn at Teffont near Salisbury, illustrated above. Most have worked with the Frith Collection for many years. All have in common one quality: they have a passion for the Frith Collection. The team is constantly expanding, but currently includes:

Paul Baron, Jason Buck, John Buck, Heather Crisp, David Davies, Louis du Mont, Isobel Hall, Lucy Hart, Julian Hight, Peter Horne, James Kinnear, Karen Kinnear, Tina Leary, Stuart Login, Sue Molloy, Miles Murray, Sarah Roberts, Kate Rotondetto, Dean Scource, Eliza Sackett, Terence Sackett, Sandra Sampson, Adrian Sanders, Sandra Sanger, Julia Skinner, Lewis Taylor, Shelley Tolcher, Lorraine Tuck, Miranda Tunnicliffe, David Turner and Ricky Williams.